Save Your Marriage

Master Effective Communication With Your Husband

(The Secret to Breaking the Conflict Cycle in Your Marriage)

Robert Fortin

Published By **Frank Joseph**

Robert Fortin

All Rights Reserved

Save Your Marriage: Master Effective Communication With Your Husband (The Secret to Breaking the Conflict Cycle in Your Marriage)

ISBN 978-1-7781779-7-2

No part of this guidebook shall be reproduced in any form without permission in writing from the publisher except in the case of brief quotations embodied in critical articles or reviews.

Legal & Disclaimer

The information contained in this book is not designed to replace or take the place of any form of medicine or professional medical advice. The information in this book has been provided for educational & entertainment purposes only.

The information contained in this book has been compiled from sources deemed reliable, and it is accurate to the best of the Author's knowledge; however, the Author cannot guarantee its accuracy and validity and cannot be held liable for any errors or omissions. Changes are periodically made to this book. You must consult your doctor or get professional medical advice before using any of the suggested remedies, techniques, or information in this book.

Upon using the information contained in this book, you agree to hold harmless the Author from and against any damages, costs, and expenses, including any legal fees potentially resulting from the application of any of the information provided by this guide. This disclaimer applies to any damages or injury caused by the use and application, whether directly or indirectly, of any advice or information presented, whether for breach of contract, tort, negligence, personal injury, criminal intent, or under any other cause of action.

You agree to accept all risks of using the information presented inside this book. You need to consult a professional medical practitioner in order to ensure you are both able and healthy enough to participate in this program.

Table Of Contents

Chapter 1: Recognizing the Warning Signs 1

Chapter 2: Unpacking the Root Causes of Marital Issues 7

Chapter 3: Effective Communication Strategies 15

Chapter 4: Restoring Emotional Intimacy 23

Chapter 5: Healing From Infidelity and Betrayal 34

Chapter 6: Managing Stress 44

Chapter 7: Fostering A Strong Partnership 55

Chapter 8: Seeking Professional Help 63

Chapter 9: Understanding the Importance of Marriage 73

Chapter 10: Identifying Signs of Marital Issues....................................... 86

Chapter 11: Nurturing A Healthy Relationship 95

Chapter 12: Addressing Specific Marital Issues 107

Chapter 13: Dealing With Infidelity and Rebuilding Trust 118

Chapter 14: Building a Shared Vision and Goals 135

Chapter 15: Relationship-Building Activities 153

Chapter 16: Understanding Why Your Marriage Is Failing 158

Chapter 17: Taking Action to Save Your Marriage 174

Chapter 1: Recognizing The Warning Signs

Section 1.1: Identifying Communication Breakdowns and Emotional Distance

In any marriage, powerful communiqué and emotional connection are crucial. When those factors start to go to pot, it can be an early caution signal that you're courting goes through demanding conditions. Recognizing communiqué breakdowns and emotional distance is essential for statistics America of your marriage and taking proactive steps to address them.

1.1.1 Lack of Open and Honest Communication

One of the primary signs of conversation breakdown is a loss of open and honest communicates among partners. You can also additionally furthermore find that conversations emerge as superficial or complete of anxiety, or essential subjects are prevented altogether. Communication breakdowns can purpose misunderstandings, unresolved conflicts, and a developing revel in of distance.

Pay hobby to signs and signs and symptoms and symptoms which include not unusual arguments, passive-competitive behavior, or reluctance to proportion mind and feelings. If you test a pattern of keeping off hard conversations or feeling unheard, it could be an instance that communication for your marriage needs interest.

1.1.2 Emotional Withdrawal and Disconnection

Emotional distance in a marriage can display up in numerous procedures. You or your associate might also additionally furthermore start to revel in emotionally indifferent, leading to a revel in of loneliness or a loss of emotional useful resource. You would possibly find yourselves spending much less incredible time collectively or conducting sports and hobbies one by one, in addition widening the emotional hollow.

Take be aware about modifications in intimacy and affection, which incorporates a lower in physical closeness, loss of shared interests, or a mean feeling of disconnection. Emotional withdrawal can erode the foundation of your marriage, making it important to address the ones issues proper away.

1.1.Three Loss of Trust and Secrecy

Trust office work the bedrock of a healthful marriage. When bear in mind starts offevolved offevolved to erode, it can have a large impact on the general state of your courting. Look for signs and signs and symptoms of secrecy or a loss of get hold of as actual with, which includes hiding financial statistics, maintaining secrets and strategies, or assignment behaviors that breach the consider of your accomplice.

Dishonesty, whether or not or no longer massive or small, can undermine the inspiration of acquire as genuine with amongst companions. If you take a look at a pattern of deception or a breakdown in do not forget, it's miles critical to address those problems brazenly and in reality.

1.1. Four Changes in Emotional Intimacy

Emotional intimacy is a key issue of a fulfilling marriage. When emotional intimacy wanes, it could purpose emotions of disconnection and dissatisfaction. Pay interest to adjustments in the diploma of emotional intimacy among you and your companion.

You also can moreover be conscious a decrease in open sharing of mind and feelings, a lack of empathy, or a revel in of emotional guardedness. These adjustments can create a barrier amongst you and your accomplice, making it essential to discover the reasons behind the shift in emotional intimacy.

Recognizing the ones warning signs and signs and symptoms and signs and symptoms is step one in assessing the dominion of your marriage. By acknowledging the communication breakdowns and emotional distance, you could begin to deal with the underlying issues and work inside the direction of rebuilding a stronger, greater related dating.

Section 1.2: Assessing the Level of Trust and Intimacy in Your Relationship

Trust and intimacy are vital elements of a strong and fulfilling marriage. Assessing the quantity of accept as true with and intimacy to your courting is critical to understanding the overall health and dynamics of your partnership. By truly comparing those additives, you may gain insights into regions that might want development and take steps inside the direction of rebuilding a strong foundation.

1.2.1 Trust Assessment

Trust is the cornerstone of any healthy courting. To test the volume of consider to your marriage, do not forget the subsequent questions:

1. Do you and your companion sense cushty being open and sincere with every one-of-a-type?

2. Are there any unresolved consider problems from the beyond that hold to have an impact in your dating?

3. Do you've got self warranty on your partner's reliability and dependability?

four. Are there any secrets and techniques and techniques or hidden behaviors that erode receive as true with between you and your companion?

five. Are both partners dedicated to rebuilding and maintaining accept as actual with?

Chapter 2: Unpacking The Root Causes Of Marital Issues

Section 2.1: Exploring Common Issues Leading to Divorce

In order to address the demanding situations on your marriage and artwork in the direction of rebuilding acquire as real with, it is essential to understand the basis reasons of the issues you are going thru. By exploring the commonplace issues that often bring about divorce, you may advantage perception into the correct areas that could require interest and find out techniques to conquer them.

2.1.1 Poor Communication

One of the maximum regular troubles in marriages is terrible communication. This can display up in numerous strategies, which incorporates useless listening, commonplace arguments, loss of recognize, and an lack of capability to explicit one's desires and problems openly. Poor verbal exchange can reason misunderstandings, resentment, and emotional distance amongst companions.

To address lousy conversation, it's far essential to boom energetic listening capabilities, exercise empathy, and create a solid space for open and honest speak. Couples can benefit from getting to know powerful communique strategies, which encompass the use of "I" statements, avoiding blame, and looking for to apprehend every superb's views.

2.1.2 Lack of Trust and Infidelity

Trust workplace paintings the foundation of a wholesome marriage. When be given as true with is damaged or lacking, it may have a profound effect on the relationship. Infidelity is one of the most devastating breaches of bear in mind and is usually a fundamental cause of divorce. However, agree with problems can also stem from distinctive factors, which consist of secrecy, dishonesty, or a records of broken guarantees.

Rebuilding take transport of as actual with requires strength of mind, transparency, and regular strive from each companions. It might also additionally comprise seeking out expert assist, task open and honest conversations, and taking steps to rebuild consider progressively through the years. Couples can gain from setting clear expectancies, establishing obstacles, and going for walks within the direction of forgiveness and healing.

2.1. Three Financial Conflicts

Money-related troubles are a commonplace supply of marital pressure. Disagreements approximately spending conduct, financial desires, or unequal contributions to own family finances can create tension and battle. Financial strain and disagreements can result in a breakdown in keep in mind, communique troubles, and a revel in of instability in the relationship.

To address financial conflicts, couples can artwork on developing a shared statistics of financial values and goals. This can also moreover moreover encompass developing a price range, exploring joint desire-making techniques, and searching out professional recommendation if important. Open and sincere communique about monetary topics, similarly to a willingness to compromise and find out commonplace ground, can assist alleviate the ones conflicts.

2.1.Four Lack of Intimacy and Emotional Connection

Intimacy and emotional connection are important for a thriving marriage. When couples enjoy a lack of intimacy, whether or not physical, emotional, or intellectual, it could bring about emotions of dissatisfaction, loneliness, and disconnection. Over time, this can erode the inspiration of the relationship and make a contribution to marital issues.

To address a loss of intimacy, couples can interest on nurturing emotional connection thru first-rate time together, open communication, and shared activities. It is vital to prioritize the bodily and emotional dreams of both partners, have interaction in honest conversations about goals and obstacles, and are in search of for expert guidance if vital.

By exploring those commonplace issues predominant to divorce, you could benefit a better understanding of the best annoying conditions for your marriage. Remember, every relationship is specific, and it is essential to method those issues with empathy, patience, and a willingness to art work together as a collection.

Section 2.2: Addressing Patterns of Conflict and Resentment

In many marriages, styles of struggle and resentment can become entrenched over time, most important to full-size pressure on the relationship. It is critical to address those styles and discover ways to solve struggle constructively, fostering a extra in shape and greater harmonious partnership. By recognizing and addressing styles of warfare and resentment, you may work closer to rebuilding endure in thoughts and developing a greater satisfactory marital dynamic.

2.2.1 Recognizing Patterns of Conflict

Patterns of war frequently emerge whilst humans time and again engage in terrible verbal exchange behaviors and techniques. These patterns can encompass common arguments, yelling, blaming, stonewalling, or task passive-competitive conduct. It is vital to understand those patterns and apprehend the effect they've got on the connection.

Take the time to mirror on the routine conflicts in your marriage. Identify the triggers, the perfect behaviors or responses that usually commonly generally tend to expand conflicts, and the underlying emotions that fuel those patterns. By gaining focus of these styles, you could begin to break the cycle and locate more wholesome approaches to talk and clear up conflicts.

2.2.2 Developing Healthy Conflict Resolution Skills

Effective conflict decision is important for a wholesome marriage. It includes locating at the equal time useful answers and addressing disagreements in a respectful and optimistic manner. Here are a few techniques to help you make bigger healthy struggle desire competencies:

a. Active Listening: Practice energetic listening with the useful resource of giving your complete hobby for your companion, looking for to recognize their perspective, and validating their feelings and troubles.

b. Use "I" Statements: Express your very very own feelings and wishes using "I" statements, keeping off blame or complaint. This permits foster a non-confrontational and much a great deal less protective environment.

c. Take Breaks: If a warfare becomes heated, follow take a ruin and revisit the talk even as you every have had time to chill out and collect your thoughts.

d. Seek Compromise: Look for answers that meet the desires of each companions. Be inclined to make concessions and discover a center ground that lets in for mutual delight.

e. Practice Empathy: Seek to recognize your accomplice's emotions and emotions, even if you disagree with their mind-set. Empathy permits create an surroundings of facts and fosters emotional connection.

2.2.Three Addressing Resentment

Resentment can boom over the years even as conflicts and issues skip unresolved. It is critical to cope with and clear up underlying resentments to save you them from further unfavourable the connection. Here are some steps to cope with resentment:

a. Open Communication: Create a safe region for open and honest verbal exchange. Express your feelings of resentment flippantly and actually, and take note of your companion's mindset with empathy.

b. Identify Triggers: Understand an appropriate behaviors, conditions, or events that cause emotions of resentment. This reputation assist you to and your companion avoid or cope with those triggers proactively.

c. Practice Forgiveness: Forgiveness can be a effective tool for liberating resentment. Work on forgiving your companion for past hurts, and additionally exercising self-forgiveness for any function you can have achieved in perpetuating the terrible cycle.

d. Seek Professional Help: If addressing resentment proves hard, don't forget seeking out the steering of a couples therapist or counselor who can offer greater help and gear for choice.

Remember that addressing styles of war and resentment takes time and effort from each partner. It calls for a dedication to open conversation, empathy, and a willingness to trade terrible behaviors.

Chapter 3: Effective Communication Strategies

Section 3.1: Active Listening and Empathy

Effective verbal exchange is the cornerstone of a wholesome and thriving dating. It includes not nice expressing oneself genuinely but additionally actively listening and empathizing collectively with your partner. By operating toward lively listening and empathy, you could foster expertise, assemble trust, and beef up your connection with your accomplice.

three.1.1 The Importance of Active Listening

Active listening is a abilties that lets in you to honestly engage together with your associate and display your right interest in their thoughts, emotions, and issues. It includes giving your undivided hobby, postponing judgment, and growing a aware try to understand their perspective. Here are a few key mind of lively listening:

1. Give Your Full Attention: When your associate is speakme, remove distractions and recognition simply on them. Maintain eye touch, nod to expose attentiveness, and keep away from interrupting.

2. Suspend Judgment: Refrain from forming critiques or making assumptions earlier. Instead, try to understand your accomplice's factor of view without right away providing counterarguments.

3. Reflect and Clarify: Summarize or paraphrase what your companion has said to make sure which you have understood correctly. This demonstrates which you are actively engaged within the communique and attempting to find clarification while wanted.

four. Validate Emotions: Acknowledge and validate your companion's emotions. Let them apprehend that their emotions are legitimate and that you empathize with what they may be experiencing.

five. Ask Open-Ended Questions: Encourage your partner to tough thru asking open-ended questions that can't be spoke back with a smooth "nice" or "no." This allows to deepen the verbal exchange and encourages your companion to percentage greater.

By schooling active listening, you create a strong area for open and full-size communique, fostering a deeper connection among you and your partner.

three.1.2 The Power of Empathy

Empathy is the capability to apprehend and percent the feelings of each other person. It goes beyond sympathy, because it calls so one can immerse yourself to your accomplice's emotional enjoy. When you precise right empathy, you display which you care about your partner's nicely-being and are willing to assist them emotionally. Here are some approaches to cultivate empathy:

1. Put Yourself in Their Shoes: Imagine how you will enjoy in case you had been in your companion's situation. This allows you benefit attitude and higher apprehend their emotions.

2. Validate Their Feelings: Let your partner realize that their emotions are valid and which you apprehend why they might be

experiencing them. Avoid dismissing or minimizing their emotions.

three. Practice Emotional Regulation: Manage your very very personal emotional reactions and avoid turning into protecting or reactive at the same time as your partner stocks their emotions. Stay calm and targeted, although the communication becomes hard or uncomfortable.

4. Use Reflective Statements: Reflect decrease returned your records of your companion's feelings and testimonies. For instance, you may say, "It looks as if you experience frustrated due to the truth..."

five. Show Support: Offer consolation and reassurance on your accomplice. Let them recognize that you are there for them and which you are dedicated to taking walks via traumatic situations collectively.

When you continually exercising empathy, you create a deeper emotional connection with your partner, fostering a sense of take delivery of as actual with, knowledge, and mutual aid.

three.1.3 Enhancing Communication Through Active Listening and Empathy

By combining active listening and empathy, you may decorate your communique capabilities and supply a lift on your courting. Here's the way to mix the ones practices:

1. Create a Safe Space: Establish an surroundings wherein each you and your partner revel in comfortable expressing yourselves openly. Encourage every special to speak definitely and pay hobby attentively.

2. Practice Mindfulness: Be present within the second all through conversations together with your companion. Avoid distractions, collectively with smartphones or specific gadgets, and in fact popularity on what they're saying.

3. Validate and Acknowledge: Respond for your associate's mind, emotions, and issues with empathy and expertise. Validate their

evaluations and feelings, regardless of the truth that you couldn't in fact trust them.

4. Avoid Defensive Behaviors: If your partner expresses some factor that triggers defensiveness in you, take a second to pause, breathe, and remind yourself to pay interest and empathize. Responding defensively can avoid powerful conversation and connection.

5. Seek Clarification and Feedback: If you are uncertain about a few detail your accomplice has stated, ask for clarification. This suggests which you are in reality interested by information their mind-set and fosters a deeper connection.

Remember, effective communique is an ongoing workout that calls for strive and dedication from each partners. By always enforcing active listening and empathy for your interactions, you could create a foundation of consider, deliver a lift to your connection, and navigate disturbing situations greater successfully.

Section 3.2: Constructive Conflict Resolution Techniques

Conflict is a herbal part of any courting, at the aspect of marriages. However, how couples cope with warfare can drastically impact the fitness and durability in their courting. Constructive struggle desire techniques offer a framework for coping with disagreements in a respectful and effective manner. By the use of those strategies, couples can address conflicts efficiently, enhance their bond, and discover collectively outstanding answers.

Chapter 4: Restoring Emotional Intimacy

Section four.1: Rekindling Romance and Passion in Your Marriage

Emotional intimacy is a critical thing of a satisfying and lengthy-lasting marriage. It consists of a deep connection, remember, and a feel of closeness among companions. However, over time, the initial spark and exhilaration can fade, and couples may additionally additionally additionally find out themselves longing to rekindle the romance and passion they as soon as had. In this section, we can discover techniques to help you reignite the flame and cultivate emotional intimacy on your marriage.

4.1.1 Prioritize Quality Time Together

One of the critical techniques to rekindle romance and ardour is with the resource of prioritizing great time together. In the busyness of regular life, it's far smooth for couples to get stuck up in responsibilities and overlook their dating. Carving out committed time for every distinct allows you to reconnect and deepen your emotional bond. Consider the following suggestions:

1. Schedule Dates: Set apart sure time for dates or sports that you each revel in. Whether it's miles a romantic dinner, a stroll within the park, or a shared interest, prioritize spending uninterrupted time collectively.

2. Unplug and Be Present: During your outstanding time, positioned away distractions collectively with phones, laptops, and the television. Focus on every one among a type, interact in significant conversations, and enjoy each distinct's business corporation.

3. Explore New Experiences: Inject novelty into your courting via attempting new sports activities sports or adventures together. This can reignite the feel of exhilaration and create shared recollections.

4. Practice Active Appreciation: Express gratitude and appreciation on your associate often. Acknowledge their efforts, strengths,

and the characteristics you adore approximately them. This fosters a super and loving surroundings for your marriage.

4.1.2 Foster Emotional Connection and Open Communication

Strong emotional intimacy requires open and honest communique. It entails sharing your mind, emotions, desires, and fears along with your accomplice and growing a constant area for vulnerability. Consider the subsequent techniques:

1. Deepen Conversations: Move past floor-degree discussions and engage in giant conversations. Ask open-ended questions, actively pay attention, and encourage your companion to percent their thoughts and emotions.

2. Share Your Dreams and Goals: Discuss your person and shared goals and aspirations. Support every different's aspirations and learn how to paintings together in the direction of your desires.

3. Practice Active Listening: As discussed in phase 3.1.1, actively concentrate in your companion without judgment, validate their emotions, and display empathy. This fosters a experience of records and connection.

4. Cultivate Emotional Trust: Create an surroundings wherein each partners revel in stable to unique their feelings and vulnerabilities with out worry of judgment or grievance. Trust is the foundation of emotional intimacy.

four.1.Three Nurture Physical Intimacy

Physical intimacy is an vital element of a romantic dating, and nurturing it may assist reignite ardour and deepen emotional connection. Consider the following tips:

1. Prioritize Affection: Engage in small bodily gestures of affection consisting of preserving arms, hugging, kissing, or cuddling. These acts of intimacy can support the emotional bond among companions.

2. Explore Sensuality: Take time to discover and apprehend every distinct's desires and needs. Experiment with new evaluations, learn how to please and fulfill each other, and prioritize mutual satisfaction.

three. Communicate About Sexual Intimacy: Openly speak your desires, boundaries, and expectations concerning sexual intimacy. Regularly check in with every special to ensure each companions enjoy heard and satisfied.

4. Seek Professional Help if Needed: If physical intimacy has end up a supply of anxiety or task on your dating, undergo in thoughts looking for guidance from a therapist or counselor who makes a speciality of couples' intimacy.

Remember, rekindling romance and ardour takes attempt and strength of mind from each companions. It calls for open verbal exchange, exquisite time collectively, and a willingness to discover and meet each unique's goals. By prioritizing emotional connection, nurturing physical intimacy, and fostering open communique, you can repair and deepen the bond for your marriage.

Section four.2: Building Emotional Bridges and Deepening Your Connection

Emotional intimacy is the muse of a sturdy and satisfying marriage. It consists of deepening your emotional connection and records collectively with your companion. In this segment, we can find out strategies that will help you assemble emotional bridges and deepen your connection.

4.2.1 Practice Empathy and Understanding

Empathy is the functionality to apprehend and proportion the emotions of some other character. It plays a essential function in constructing emotional bridges and fostering a deeper connection with your associate. Consider the following techniques:

1. Put Yourself in Their Shoes: Make a conscious attempt to look the state of affairs out of your accomplice's angle. Try to

apprehend their feelings, thoughts, and underlying needs. This allow you to reply with compassion and manual.

2. Validate Their Feelings: Acknowledge and validate your associate's emotions, even if you do now not typically do not forget them. Let them recognize that their feelings are valid and crucial to you.

3. Reflective Listening: Practice reflective listening with the beneficial useful resource of paraphrasing and summarizing what your accomplice says. This demonstrates which you are actively engaged and interested by information their point of view.

4. Show Empathetic Body Language: Non-verbal cues which include retaining eye touch, nodding, and the usage of open and inviting frame language can deliver empathy and information.

four.2.2 Share Vulnerabilities and Deepen Trust

Sharing vulnerabilities is an crucial part of constructing emotional intimacy. It calls for receive as true with and a willingness to be open and sincere together collectively with your associate. Consider the subsequent strategies:

1. Create a Safe Space: Foster an environment wherein each partners enjoy stable to percent their vulnerabilities without worry of judgment or complaint. Establish take delivery of as real with via manner of using responding with compassion and useful useful resource.

2. Share Your Inner World: Open up approximately your thoughts, fears, hopes, and desires. Allow your associate to look the depths of your emotions and mind, as this will create a stronger emotional connection.

3. Practice Emotional Risk-Taking: Take small steps in sharing deeper feelings and reviews on the aspect of your partner. As you each turn out to be greater comfortable, frequently

increase the extent of vulnerability to your conversations.

4. Build Trust Through Consistency: Consistently show trustworthiness through keeping your guarantees, being dependable, and following via on commitments. This allows create a stable basis for emotional intimacy.

four.2.Three Cultivate Gratitude and Appreciation

Expressing gratitude and appreciation on your associate can provide a boost on your emotional bond. It fosters a amazing surroundings and allows every partners sense valued and loved. Consider the subsequent strategies:

1. Daily Appreciation: Make it a addiction to specific gratitude and appreciation in your accomplice each day. Focus on their functions, actions, and efforts which you really recognize and price.

2. Express Specific Appreciation: Be precise to your expressions of appreciation. Instead of a common "thanks," element out the proper moves or behaviors that you apprehend.

3. Surprise Gestures: Surprise your companion with small acts of kindness and thoughtfulness to illustrate your appreciation. These may be as clean as leaving a heartfelt observe or getting ready their desired meal.

4.2.Four Cultivate Shared Meaning and Rituals

Creating shared which means and rituals can deepen your emotional connection and toughen your bond as a pair. Consider the subsequent practices:

1. Establish Relationship Rituals: Develop rituals or traditions which can be unique to your relationship. These may be weekly date nights, annual holidays, or each day rituals collectively with sharing food or bedtime sporting events.

2. Identify Shared Values and Goals: Explore your shared values, beliefs, and prolonged-

term dreams as a couple. Discuss how you may artwork together to meet those aspirations and create a sizeable lifestyles together.

3. Support Each Other's Growth: Encourage and useful resource every different's private increase and individual aspirations. Celebrate every exclusive's achievements and provide emotional assist at some stage in hard instances.

Building emotional bridges and deepening your connection is an ongoing technique that requires strive and commitment. By going for walks in the direction of empathy, sharing vulnerabilities, cultivating gratitude, and creating shared because of this, you can make more potent the emotional bond for your marriage and experience a deeper revel in of achievement and connection.

Chapter 5: Healing From Infidelity And Betrayal

Section five.1: Navigating the Challenges of Rebuilding Trust after an Affair

Infidelity and betrayal can be devastating to a wedding, causing deep emotional wounds and eroding accepts as real with. However, with strength of will and attempt from every partners, it's miles viable to heal and rebuild believe. In this segment, we're able to find out techniques to assist navigate the worrying situations of rebuilding receive as true with after an affair.

5.1.1 Acknowledge and Address the Emotions

After the discovery of an affair, every partners will in all likelihood enjoy some of intense emotions which incorporates anger, harm, betrayal, and disappointment. It is vital to famend and address the ones feelings to start the recovery way. Consider the following steps:

1. Allow Time for Grieving: Both companions want time to technique the ache and emotions related to the affair. Give yourself permission to grieve and specific your feelings in a wholesome and constructive way.

2. Seek Individual Support: Consider looking for individual treatment or counseling to help you navigate your emotions and benefit insights into the effect of the affair to your existence and well-being.

three. Communicate Openly: Create a safe area for open and sincere verbal exchange together along with your accomplice. Express your emotions, issues, and goals, and inspire your associate to do the same. This can facilitate expertise and empathy.

five.1.2 Commit to Transparency and Accountability

Rebuilding take into account calls for a willpower to transparency and responsibility from the associate who had the affair. Consider the subsequent steps:

1. Complete Disclosure: The untrue associate want to be inclined to offer an entire and sincere account of the affair, answering any questions the betrayed accomplice may additionally moreover have. This transparency is vital for rebuilding undergo in thoughts.

2. Establish Boundaries: Both companions have to agree on clear limitations to prevent future breaches of accept as true with. This may additionally additionally encompass placing recommendations for verbal exchange, social interactions, or maintaining transparency in non-public subjects.

three. Consistent Honesty: The untrue partner wishes to demonstrate constant honesty in all factors of the connection. Small lies or omissions can erode accept as true with, so it is vital to prioritize honesty and integrity.

five.1.Three Rebuilding Trust Through Actions

Rebuilding recollect is a gradual way that requires steady try and moves. Consider the subsequent strategies:

1. Keep Promises: The untrue associate want to make a conscious try to maintain their ensures and examine via on commitments. This demonstrates reliability and builds consider through the years.

2. Show Remorse and Empathy: The unfaithful accomplice have to specific true regret for their movements, displaying empathy for the pain they have got caused. This can help the betrayed accomplice enjoy heard and understood.

3. Consistency and Reliability: Consistently show trustworthiness thru moves and conduct. This includes being punctual, dependable, and responsible in all components of the relationship.

5.1.Four Seek Professional Help

Recovering from infidelity can be a complicated and difficult way. Consider looking for the guidance of a certified therapist or counselor who specializes in couples treatment. They can offer a safe and unbiased vicinity for each partners to specific their emotions and work via the disturbing conditions of rebuilding recall.

Additionally, expert assist can offer precious insights, gear, and strategies to facilitate the recovery machine and assist each companions navigate the complexities of rebuilding remember after an affair.

Rebuilding endure in thoughts after an affair is an prolonged and tough journey. It calls for staying strength, information, and a determination to growth from every partners. With time, effort, and expert useful resource, it's far possible to heal the accidents, rebuild accept as true with, and create a more potent and greater resilient marriage.

Section 5.2: Establishing Boundaries and Repairing the Relationship

After the invention of an affair, establishing obstacles and repairing the relationship come to be important steps in rebuilding don't forget and growing a extra fit dynamic. In this segment, we're capable of discover strategies that will help you navigate this system.

five.2.1 Establish Clear and Healthy Boundaries

Setting easy and healthful barriers is vital for rebuilding take into account and keeping a regular courting. Consider the following steps:

1. Open Communication: Engage in open and sincere communique together together along with your companion to set up limitations that every of you're snug with. This may additionally moreover moreover include discussing expectancies spherical constancy, privateness, and private region.

2. Define Relationship Agreements: Together, define specific relationship agreements that define appropriate conduct and moves. These agreements need to be collectively agreed

upon and revered via manner of manner of each companions.

3. Rebuild Privacy and Transparency: Determine the volume of privacy and transparency that feels snug for each partners. This can also additionally comprise sharing passwords, being open approximately social interactions, or rebuilding accept as true with in considered one of a type regions in which it have become damaged.

five.2.2 Foster Emotional Safety and Vulnerability

Creating emotional protection and fostering vulnerability are essential for repairing the connection after an affair. Consider the subsequent strategies:

1. Practice Active Listening: Listen attentively in your accomplice without judgment or defensiveness. Create a secure location for them to unique their emotions, issues, and dreams.

2. Express Empathy and Understanding: Show empathy and statistics within the path of your partner's emotions and studies. Validate their feelings and reveal a true desire to apprehend and useful aid them.

3. Share Vulnerabilities: Both companions have to be willing to percentage their vulnerabilities and be open approximately their non-public emotional goals and insecurities. This can foster empathy and deepen the emotional connection.

five.2.Three Rebuilding Intimacy and Connection

Rebuilding intimacy and connection is a vital a part of repairing the relationship. Consider the subsequent strategies:

1. Cultivate Emotional Intimacy: Engage in sports that sell emotional intimacy, together with mission deep conversations, sharing goals and aspirations, and expressing appreciation and love for each precise.

2. **Prioritize Quality Time:** Set aside committed super time for each unique to rebuild the relationship. This can consist of date nights, weekend getaways, or undertaking shared pursuits and pastimes.

3. **Seek Professional Help:** Consider attempting to find the assist of a licensed therapist or counselor who specializes in couples remedy. They can provide steering and assist in rebuilding intimacy and connection and assist navigate the complexities of the recovery process.

5.2.Four Practice Forgiveness and Letting Go

Forgiveness plays a vital role inside the restoration approach after an affair. Consider the following strategies:

1. **Understand the Process:** Recognize that forgiveness is a device that takes time and varies for every character. It does no longer advise forgetting or condoning the affair however rather liberating the horrible feelings and moving toward recuperation.

2. Seek Support: Engage in character remedy or counseling that will help you method the ache, anger, and resentment related to the affair. A therapist can manual you through the forgiveness approach and offer equipment that will help you allow move of terrible emotions.

three. Rebuilding Trust: Forgiveness and remember move hand in hand. As take delivery of as actual with is rebuilt through ordinary moves and transparency, it will become less difficult to allow move of the pain and circulate towards forgiveness.

Rebuilding a dating after an affair is a difficult and complex way. It requires dedication, persistence, and a willingness to confront tough feelings. By putting in barriers, fostering emotional protection, rebuilding intimacy, and working towards forgiveness, you can art work within the path of repairing the connection and developing a stronger and greater resilient partnership.

Chapter 6: Managing Stress

Section 6.1: Strategies for Reducing Stress and Sharing Responsibilities

In a healthful marriage, handling stress and balancing responsibilities are essential for maintaining harmony and properly-being. Life can be worrying, but via enforcing effective strategies, couples can reduce pressure stages and percent duties more correctly. In this phase, we are able to find out techniques that will help you gain a greater in shape stability.

6.1.1 Prioritize Self-Care

Self-care is crucial for handling stress and preserving ordinary nicely-being. When you deal with yourself, you're better ready to cope with the needs of each day lifestyles and aid your companion. Consider the subsequent self-care strategies:

1. Physical Health: Prioritize normal exercise, eat a balanced weight loss plan, and get sufficient sleep. Taking care of your bodily

health contributes to better strain manipulate and fundamental properly-being.

2. Emotional Well-being: Engage in sports that promote emotional properly-being, which consist of journaling, operating towards mindfulness or meditation, and pursuing hobbies or pastimes that supply you pleasure and relaxation.

three. Time for Yourself: Carve out devoted time for yourself to recharge and pursue sports activities activities that you experience. This may be analyzing a ebook, taking a tub, going for a stroll, or sporting out some other hobby that enables you lighten up and rejuvenate.

6.1.2 Open and Honest Communication

Effective conversation is critical for handling strain and sharing obligations in a marriage. Open and honest communication allows every partners to explicit their goals, worries, and expectations. Consider the subsequent communication techniques:

1. Regular Check-Ins: Set apart time for everyday take a look at-ins in conjunction with your accomplice wherein you may speak your person stressors, demanding situations, and duties. This can assist make sure that each partners are aware of each different's desires and might offer help whilst important.

2. Active Listening: Practice energetic listening via way of way of attentively paying attention to your associate's issues and goals without interrupting or becoming defensive. Show empathy and statistics, and validate their emotions.

3. Problem-Solving Together: Collaborate collectively together with your companion to discover answers to shared demanding situations. Brainstorm thoughts, talk capability techniques, and work collectively to discover a balance that works for each of you.

6.1.Three Delegate and Share Responsibilities

Sharing duties is crucial to retaining off an outstanding burden on one partner and fostering a experience of equality in the courting. Consider the following strategies:

1. Identify Strengths and Interests: Identify every accomplice's strengths, pursuits, and alternatives on the subject of one-of-a-kind duties. Delegate obligations consequently, thinking of all people's abilties and alternatives.

2. Create a Task List: Make a list of all of the circle of relatives obligations, monetary duties, and other responsibilities. Divide them fairly among every companions, ensuring that all people has a balanced workload.

3. Regularly Revisit and Adjust: Regularly revisit and regulate the department of responsibilities as wanted. As times trade, it can be important to redistribute duties to maintain a truthful and feasible stability.

6.1.4 Seek Support and Assistance

Don't hesitate to are searching out manual and assistance while wished. You do not must manage the whole thing in your very personal. Consider the subsequent avenues for assist:

1. Family and Friends: Reach out to circle of relatives and friends for manual and assistance at the same time as important. They can provide a listening ear, provide guidance, or assist with unique responsibilities.

2. Professional Help: If pressure will become overwhelming or you're suffering to discover a healthful stability, do not forget on the lookout for the resource of a therapist or counselor. They can offer guidance, device, and strategies to control pressure successfully and navigate stressful situations on your marriage.

three. Supportive Networks: Join guide organizations or groups in which you could connect with others who can be experiencing comparable disturbing conditions. Sharing testimonies and advice can offer treasured insights and assist.

By prioritizing self-care, fostering open conversation, sharing duties, and searching out assist whilst wanted, you can reduce stress degrees and benefit a greater fit balance for your marriage. Remember that coping with pressure and balancing obligations is an ongoing way, and it is able to require ordinary modifications as activities change. With a collaborative and supportive technique, you can navigate those challenges collectively and maintain a healthy and fascinating marriage.

Section 6.2: Prioritizing Self-Care and Maintaining a Healthy Work-Life Balance

In ultra-modern speedy-paced and disturbing international, prioritizing self-care and keeping a wholesome art work-existence stability is crucial for conventional nicely-being and the achievement of your marriage. Neglecting self-care and allowing paintings to consume your existence can result in progressed strain, relationship strain, and a decline in happiness. In this phase, we're able to find out techniques that will help you prioritize self-care and collect a more in shape art work-existence balance.

6.2.1 Recognize the Importance of Self-Care

Self-care isn't egocentric; it's miles an crucial detail of preserving your bodily, emotional, and intellectual properly-being. When you cope with yourself, you're higher organized to address the responsibilities and needs of your private and expert life. Consider the subsequent techniques for prioritizing self-care:

1. Identify Self-Care Activities: Reflect on sports activities that supply you satisfaction, relaxation, and rejuvenation. This ought to include exercising, pursuits, spending time in nature, studying, meditation, or some thing else that promotes your well-being.

2. Schedule Regular Self-Care Time: Set apart dedicated time for self-care sports on your time table. Treat this time as non-negotiable

and decide to it just as you will with each different critical self-discipline.

3. Communicate Your Needs: Clearly speak your self-care needs and obstacles for your accomplice, circle of relatives, and buddies. Help them understand the significance of self-care in keeping your stylish properly-being and are looking for for their resource and statistics.

6.2.2 Establish Boundaries amongst Work and Personal Life

Creating smooth boundaries amongst paintings and private life is essential for keeping a healthy artwork-life stability. When artwork spills over into your personal lifestyles, it can lead to stress, burnout, and pressure on your relationships. Consider the following strategies for setting up boundaries:

1. Define Work Hours: Set specific artwork hours and try to stay with them as lots as feasible. Clearly speak the ones hours on your colleagues, clients, and superiors, and avoid

carrying out art work-related obligations outdoor of those particular hours.

2. Create Physical Separation: Designate specific regions for artwork and private life. If viable, have a separate place of business vicinity or workspace where you can interest on art work. This bodily separation can help create a intellectual boundary among artwork and personal lifestyles.

three. Turn Off Work Notifications: Disconnect from paintings-associated notifications and emails inside the course of your personal time. Set clean limitations on the side of your paintings gadgets and establish instances at the same time as you are "off-responsibility."

6.2.Three Delegate and Prioritize Tasks

Recognize that you do not need to do everything in your very very personal. Delegating duties and prioritizing sports can help alleviate the workload and create greater time for self-care and private existence. Consider the following strategies:

1. Identify Priorities: Determine your maximum important obligations and obligations and hobby on them. Learn to distinguish among responsibilities which are absolutely important and those that may be delegated or eliminated.

2. Delegate Responsibilities: Delegate duties for your companion, circle of relatives individuals, or colleagues whilst suitable. Share the workload and duties, and apprehend that asking for help isn't a sign of weak point but a clever manner to govern some time and strength.

three. Learn to Say No: Set limitations and have a look at to say no at the same time as you're already feeling overwhelmed or even as a request does not align collectively collectively together with your priorities. Prioritize your well-being and guard it slow and electricity.

6.2. Four Regularly Assess and Adjust

Maintaining a healthy artwork-lifestyles balance is an ongoing technique that calls for normal evaluation and changes. Circumstances alternate, and what worked within the beyond may also not be powerful. Consider the following techniques:

1. Regular Self-Reflection: Take time to mirror on your work-life balance and have a look at how well you're prioritizing self-care and preserving boundaries. Ask yourself if any adjustments are needed to obtain a greater healthful stability.

2. Communicate with Your Partner: Discuss your paintings-existence balance collectively collectively together with your accomplice often. Seek their input and assist, and art work together to find answers that gain every of you and your courting.

3. Flexibility and Adaptability: Be flexible and adaptable on your technique. Recognize that undertaking a perfect art work-life balance

won't normally be possible, but strive for a balance that works for you and your precise conditions.

By prioritizing self-care, organising limitations, delegating duties, and regularly assessing and adjusting, you can accumulate a healthier work-existence balance and nurture your nicely-being and your marriage. Remember that carrying out balance is a continuous machine, and it requires aware attempt and communique. With determination and flexibility, you may create a satisfying and harmonious lifestyles that encompasses every private and expert additives.

Chapter 7: Fostering A Strong Partnership
Section 7.1: Cultivating Mutual Respect and Support

A robust partnership is constructed on a foundation of mutual recognize and manual. When each companions experience valued, understood, and supported, the relationship can thrive and resist challenges. In this phase, we are able to find out strategies for cultivating mutual understand and assist indoors your marriage.

7.1.1 Practice Active Listening

Active listening is a crucial detail of displaying apprehend and resource on your associate. It includes virtually attractive in the conversation and seeking out to recognize their mindset without judgment or interruption. Consider the subsequent techniques for operating in the direction of active listening:

1. Give Undivided Attention: When your companion is speaking, deliver them your complete interest. Put aside distractions, keep eye touch, and display actual hobby in what they're pronouncing.

2. Reflect and Validate: After your partner has expressed themselves, replicate lower back on what they have got said to make certain you understand their thoughts and feelings correctly. Validate their emotions and studies,

even though you can no longer consider their attitude.

3. Avoid Defensiveness: Resist the urge to turn out to be shielding or dismissive even as you listen a few component that may be hard or vital. Instead, technique the communique with an open mind and a willingness to apprehend your associate's perspective.

7.1.2 Practice Empathy and Understanding

Empathy is the capability to recognize and share the feelings of every other individual. By running within the course of empathy, you may create a supportive and nurturing environment interior your marriage. Consider the following techniques for cultivating empathy:

1. Put Yourself in Their Shoes: Try to anticipate what it would experience need to be for your companion's position. Consider their studies, challenges, and emotions. This thoughts-set will assist you to respond with empathy and facts.

2. Validate Their Feelings: Acknowledge and validate your partner's emotions, despite the fact that you can not completely understand or take delivery of as authentic with them. Let them understand that their emotions are valid and essential to you.

3. Offer Support and Encouragement: Show your accomplice that you are there to assist them through every the thrill and the problems of life. Offer words of encouragement, lend a helping hand, and be a deliver of energy when they need it.

7.1.Three Communicate with Respect

Respectful communication is vital for retaining a wholesome and supportive partnership. When every companions communicate with respect, it fosters an environment of protection and take transport of as right with. Consider the following techniques for speaking with respect:

1. Use "I" Statements: When expressing your thoughts or problems, use "I" statements

instead of "you" statements. This enables you take ownership of your feelings and avoids sounding accusatory or confrontational.

2. Avoid Blame and Criticism: Instead of blaming or criticizing your partner, recognition on expressing your private feelings and wishes. Use high-quality language and steer the verbal exchange closer to locating solutions instead of residing on problems.

three. Practice Kindness and Courtesy: Treat your accomplice with kindness and courtesy, even in tough situations. Avoid derogatory language, sarcasm, or belittling comments. Instead, pick out phrases that uplift and show admire.

7.1.Four Support Each Other's Goals and Dreams

Supporting each different's dreams and dreams is a essential trouble of a robust partnership. When both companions experience recommended and supported in pursuing their character aspirations, it strengthens the bond among you. Consider the following strategies for supporting each other's desires:

1. Active Interest: Show right interest for your accomplice's desires and goals. Ask questions, offer encouragement, and feature a laugh their accomplishments along the manner.

2. Emotional Support: Be a deliver of emotional aid to your partner after they face demanding situations or setbacks. Offer a listening ear, offer reassurance, and remind them of their strengths and abilties.

3. Collaboration: Explore possibilities for collaboration and mutual assist in pursuing your person dreams. Find tactics to assist every one of a kind, whether or now not it's miles via sharing sources, providing comments, or offering realistic help.

By cultivating mutual admire and aid in your marriage through energetic listening, empathy, respectful conversation, and supporting each unique's dreams, you could foster a robust partnership. Remember that building a robust partnership is an ongoing method that requires effort and commitment from each partners. With a foundation of respect and help, you may navigate demanding situations collectively and create a dating that flourishes on believe, information, and mutual growth.

Section 7.2: Collaborating on Shared Goals and Dreams

In addition to helping every other's person goals and dreams, taking part on shared dreams and desires ought to make stronger the bond and enjoy of motive within your marriage. When you discern collectively towards a commonplace vision, you create a deeper connection and a experience of shared accomplishment. In this section, we're able to find out techniques for taking part on shared desires and dreams.

7.2.1 Identify and Discuss Shared Goals

The first step in taking detail on shared dreams and dreams is to find out and communicate them brazenly collectively with your partner. Take the time to discover and recognize every awesome's aspirations, desires, and priorities. Consider the subsequent techniques:

1. Reflect Individually: Each accomplice need to make an effort for self-reflected photograph to pick out out non-public desires and desires. Consider what you want to attain in my opinion and what you envision in your partnership.

2. Share and Discuss: Come together and percent your man or woman dreams and desires with each one among a kind. Create a stable space for open and sincere verbal exchange. Listen attentively in your accomplice's aspirations and specific your own desires.

Chapter 8: Seeking Professional Help

Section 8.1: Knowing When to Seek Marriage Counseling or Therapy

Marriage counseling or remedy can be a precious beneficial useful resource for couples who are going via disturbing situations or searching out to strengthen their relationship. Recognizing whilst to attempting to find expert assistance is an essential step towards addressing issues and fostering a more fit partnership. In this phase, we are able to discover symptoms and signs and signs that advocate it may be time to bear in mind marriage counseling or remedy.

eight.1.1 Communication Breakdown

Communication is a cornerstone of a wholesome courting. If you and your associate are experiencing everyday verbal exchange breakdowns, which include not unusual misunderstandings, steady arguments, or problem expressing yourselves efficaciously, it can be beneficial to searching for professional help. A marriage counselor or therapist can provide steering and educate you effective conversation strategies to beautify your interactions.

8.1.2 Persistent Conflict

Conflict is a regular a part of any courting, however whilst conflicts become commonplace, intense, or unresolved, it could strain the partnership. If you and your companion discover yourselves caught in a cycle of repeated conflicts or in case you aren't able to find resolutions, marriage counseling or treatment can provide a steady area to discover the underlying troubles and expand more wholesome techniques to control conflicts.

8.1.Three Loss of Intimacy or Connection

Over time, couples also can additionally revel in a loss of intimacy or connection. This can show up as a loss of emotional closeness, reduced physical intimacy, or feeling disconnected from each incredible's lives. If you and your partner are struggling to reignite the spark or sense emotionally far off, a marriage counselor or therapist permit you to deal with these problems and paintings in the route of rebuilding intimacy and connection.

8.1.Four Infidelity or Betrayal

Discovering infidelity or experiencing any form of betrayal can deeply impact a relationship. Rebuilding bear in mind and healing from such wounds may be difficult with out expert steering. Marriage counseling or treatment can provide a based totally and supportive environment to cope with the aftermath of infidelity, navigate the complicated feelings worried, and artwork toward rebuilding hold in mind and forgiveness.

eight.1.Five Life Transitions or Stressors

Major lifestyles transitions or wonderful stressors can positioned pressure on a marriage. Events together with becoming dad and mom, profession changes, economic issues, or the dearth of a loved you can effect the dynamics amongst partners. If you and your associate are struggling to navigate the ones transitions or manipulate the associated stressors, seeking out expert assist can offer you with the equipment and assist needed to cope efficiently.

eight.1.6 Lack of Progress or Stagnation

If you and your accomplice have been trying to find to address courting issues on your very personal but have no longer visible big development or find yourselves stuck in patterns that are not enhancing, it may be time to attempting to find the assist of a marriage counselor or therapist. They can provide glowing perspectives, unbiased steerage, and proof-based totally techniques that will help you flow into beforehand.

8.1.7 Individual Mental Health Concerns

Individual intellectual health concerns can impact a relationship. If both you or your accomplice is experiencing full-size highbrow fitness stressful conditions, which incorporates melancholy, anxiety, dependancy, or trauma, it may have an impact on the overall properly-being of the partnership. Seeking expert assist can useful resource everybody recovery and the relationship as a whole.

Remember, searching out professional help does no longer suggest that your relationship is failing. It is a proactive step in the direction of boom, healing, and enhancing your partnership. A skilled marriage counselor or therapist can provide guidance, train powerful techniques, and facilitate open and sincere verbal exchange. They permit you to and your associate navigate annoying conditions, increase healthier styles, and create a more potent and extra excellent dating.

Section eight.2: Utilizing Support Networks and Community Resources

While attempting to find professional help through marriage counseling or treatment is beneficial, it is also important to utilize aid networks and network assets to enhance your relationship. These assets can offer extra steerage, attitude, and a experience of belonging. In this segment, we can find out techniques to faucet into resource networks and community property.

eight.2.1 Family and Friends

Your own family and buddies may be a treasured deliver of aid and steering for your dating. They can provide a listening ear, provide advice primarily based totally on their very very own reports, and offer one-of-a-kind views. Don't hesitate to achieve out to relied on cherished ones for emotional guide or to talk approximately courting disturbing conditions. However, undergo in mind that their perspectives can be subjective, so it's far essential to take into account their recommendation inside the context of your personal courting.

8.2.2 Support Groups

Support groups offer a place wherein humans can connect with others who're going through similar challenges. In the context of relationships, there are manual organizations available for numerous conditions, which embody couples dealing with infertility, parents of youngsters with particular desires, or couples in mixed families. These corporations offer a feel of community, understanding, and the opportunity to study from others' reports. Look for neighborhood help groups in your area or preserve in thoughts online businesses and forums.

8.2.Three Workshops and Retreats

Relationship workshops and retreats provide educational opportunities to study and extend collectively as a couple. These applications frequently cover topics collectively with communique competencies, war resolution, intimacy building, and dating enrichment. Participating in workshops or retreats can provide you with realistic equipment, insights, and the risk to connect to other couples who are also invested in their relationships.

eight.2.Four Online Resources

The net gives a wealth of belongings to guide your dating. Numerous web web sites, blogs, podcasts, and on line guides provide dating advice, suggestions, and bodily games that you can find out collectively. You can discover guidance on severa topics, which includes communication, intimacy, courting constructing, and hassle-fixing. However, make certain which you rely on legit assets and recollect the credibility of the statistics you come upon.

eight.2.Five Religious or Spiritual Support

If you have a non secular or spiritual affiliation, your faith network may be a precious aid for help and guidance. Many non secular companies offer marital counseling, couples' retreats, or assist agencies that align with their beliefs and values. Engaging together with your faith network can offer a enjoy of shared values and a supportive community of people who prioritize robust and healthy relationships.

eight.2.6 Professional Development

Investing in professional development as a pair can be beneficial for your courting. Consider attending seminars or conferences targeted on relationship improvement, together with those led through manner of relationship professionals or therapists. These activities provide possibilities for learning, self-meditated photograph, and boom as a couple. Additionally, you can discover books, podcasts, or on line courses authored via using using reputable dating specialists.

Remember that the usage of manual networks and community sources is prepared attempting to find steering and learning from others who've navigated comparable annoying situations. These belongings can supplement the paintings you do with a wedding counselor or therapist and offer ongoing help in the end of your relationship journey. Be open to reading from one-of-a-kind perspectives, but generally keep in mind what aligns along with your values and the proper dynamics of your relationship.

Chapter 9: Understanding The Importance Of Marriage

Marriage is a spiritual enterprise that is tremendously important in many cultures and societies all around the worldwide. It is the unions of those who observe spend their lives together and increase a basis of affection, recognize, and help.

One of the crucial factor motives for the importance of marriage is its function in forming robust households and providing conducive surroundings for infant-rearing. Children who increase up in a married family carry out better in many regions of existence, along with schooling, highbrow and physical health, and socio-emotional development, in accordance to investigate. Both mother and father' presence and resolution to each other and their children offer a revel in of protection and balance this is essential for a children's brand new properly-being.

Marriage formalizes the jail and social acknowledgment of a couple's dating. It establishes a framework for rights and responsibilities along with property rights, inheritance, clinical picks, and tax breaks. It additionally creates a guide system for couples in times of misery and lets in couples to make critical alternatives together.

Marriage furthermore has a brilliant effect on people's emotional and mental properly-being. It gives organization, intimacy, and a feel of belonging. Having a partner who is dedicated to statistics and helping each other thru lifestyles's america of americaand downs may be in particular huge and captivating. Marriage's emotional assist can help humans in dealing with obstacles, reducing strain, and selling highbrow fitness.

It additionally promotes private growth and development. Marriage's determination and obligations consist of humans making concessions, talking effectively, and growing empathy for their accomplice. These trends contribute to non-public development and the development of important life skills.

Marriage offers a platform for personal development and pushes human beings to be the finest versions of themselves.

Marriage is also crucial in society. It improves social bonding and fosters network stability. Marriages which might be wholesome and robust characteristic function fashions for others and make a contribution to society's commonplace properly-being. Marriage additionally acts as a basis for the status quo of families, which might be the important devices of society. Strong households foster a solid and supportive environment that blessings the entire community.

Marriage is important, however it is also essential to apprehend that it isn't always the simplest legitimate and satisfying way to have a widespread life. Some people can select different pathways to satisfaction and achievement, which includes cohabitation or closing single. The fee of options for those who pick out numerous routes have to now not be faded by the importance of marriage.

Finally, marriage is required for building robust households, supplying emotional and mental help, supporting private boom, and contributing to societal cohesion. It establishes a framework for crook reputation, rights, and obligations, further to a basis for personal and relational boom. While marriage is critical, it's also crucial to apprehend and apprehend amazing humans's selections. Overall, marriage is a cherished group this is quite crucial in plenty of people's lives.

Common Challenges in Marriage

Communication is a median deliver of warfare in marriage. Effective communication is important in any relationship, but it can be especially tough in a wedding wherein humans with very considered one of a kind perspectives and communication styles attempt to artwork collectively as a group. Misunderstandings, hurt sentiments, and resentment can all emerge within the absence of clean and sincere verbal exchange.

Maintaining a wholesome stability amongst distinctiveness and cohesion is any other commonplace problem in marriage. While each accomplice should have their man or woman and observe their pastimes, the couple have to additionally prioritize their dating and spend remarkable time together. Finding that stability may be tough, specifically at the same time as work, family, and extraordinary responsibilities eat a huge detail in their time and electricity.

Financial issues are every different traditional supply of battle in marriage. Managing finances as a couple can be disturbing and contentious, specially if there are variations in spending patterns, monetary dreams, or profits ranges. Couples want to have open and honest discussions about coins, set agreed dreams, and collaborate to create a finances that reflects their beliefs and priorities.

Dealing with war is some other project in marriage. Conflict is an inevitable problem of any courting, but it is able to be particularly difficult in a marriage in which there can be a robust emotional connection and a immoderate diploma of involvement. Couples can battle to find out healthful techniques to settle issues, manage disagreements, and speak their desires and feelings without jeopardizing their dating. Learning to barter struggle of phrases constructively and in a well mannered way is critical for the marriage's extended-term sustainability.

Another regular difficulty in marriage is sexual closeness. Changes in desire, numerous sexual demands, or physical fitness troubles can all have an impact on a couple's sexual connection over the years. To maintain a snug and considerable sexual courting, open and sincere communication, exploration, and a willingness to conform to each specific's converting needs are required.

Finally, juggling domestic duties is a commonplace problem in marriage. It can be hard to distribute family chores and responsibilities calmly at the same time as each couples paintings outdoor the house. Workload imbalances that cross unresolved can reason anger, frustration, and struggle in the courting. Establishing clean expectations, discussing and dispensing family obligations, and supporting every special in preserving smooth and ordered living vicinity are all important for harmony and cooperation.

Hence, marriage is not without its issues. Couples have to conquer severa hurdles to growth a a hit and lasting connection, including communique and retaining sturdy point, further to handling charge variety, resolving arguments, preserving sexual intimacy, and balancing circle of relatives responsibilities. Couples can gather their marriage and create a supportive and significant dating via figuring out those limitations and actively walking together to triumph over them.

The Impact of Divorce on Individuals and Families

Divorce has a good sized have an impact on on humans and families, influencing many factors of their lives and relationships. The ramifications of this preference is probably an prolonged way-reaching, ensuing in difficult emotional, mental, and economic upheavals.

Divorce regularly reasons a huge variety of feelings in human beings, which encompass unhappiness, rage, and sadness. Marriage breakdown can disrupt someone's experience of security and stability, essential to feelings of betrayal and unhappiness. Recognizing that their marriage has failed would possibly cause human beings to doubt their well really well worth and their capacity to create effective partnerships inside the future.

The mental effects of divorce commonly bring about prolonged strain, fear, and disappointment. Separating from a companion and transitioning to a trendy life may be an exceedingly stressful tool, mainly for folks who did no longer are searching for for the divorce. As they adjust to the changing dynamics in their lives, human beings regularly enjoy emotions of loneliness and isolation. Coping with the loss of life of a companion and the destiny that they had deliberate together may be difficult and time-eating.

Divorce has a excellent effect on children because it reasons a shift in own family family members. Children can revel in loss, confusion, and absence of self perception because of parental separation. They need to blame themselves for their parents' divorce or fear abandonment, ensuing in emotional and behavioral difficulties. Children's exercising exercises and stability may be interrupted, vital to a experience of instability and uncertainty.

Children of divorced dad and mom can also conflict with social interactions and academic success. Because of the emotional turmoil they are experiencing, they will be extra vulnerable to behavioral issues which consist of violence or withdrawal. Additionally, as children attempt to alter to the changes and cope with the emotional effect of the divorce, their academic achievements may additionally moreover lower.

Divorce often consequences in a giant upheaval within the financial situations of each people and households. Asset split and the want to useful resource precise families can positioned a burden on financial belongings. One or every couples' earning ought to decline, making it hard to keep the same tremendous of life as earlier than. Financial hassle can accentuate the emotional toll of divorce and add to the pressures.

Divorce can also destabilize the help systems on which people and families as soon as relied. Friends and extended family can also take aspects or withdraw from one or both relationships, leaving them feeling alienated and with out emotional help. Relationship breakdown also can have an effect on destiny interactions and co-parenting duties between divorced people, making it extra hard to artwork and speak effectively for the super interests of their kids.

However, it's far important to attention on that not all people and households are similarly laid low with the horrible results of divorce. Some human beings can also revel in relieved and free after the divorce, and children can also moreover modify properly to the present day family form. Individuals' and households' capability to deal with the problems of divorce can be advocated via elements which incorporates the volume of war during the divorce method, the fantastic of the co-parenting dating, and the supply of assist services.

Despite the hardships and modifications that come with divorce, many humans and families can rebuild their lives and discover happiness and contentment. Individuals can emerge stronger and extra resilient inside the aftermath of divorce, albeit it may take time, healing, and backbone to personal growth. Individuals and families can successfully navigate the impact of divorce and create a cutting-edge financial disaster of their lives with green communique, assist from friends and own family, and property for treatment and counseling.

2. Assessing the State of Your Marriage.

It is crucial in any marriage to constantly evaluation america of your relationship to make certain that it is progressing favorably. You can actively try and keep away from the painful idea of divorce via taking the time to evaluate and cope with any issues or issues.

Divorce is frequently perceived as a protracted procedure rather than an abrupt occasion. It is the cease end result of unsolved troubles, unfulfilled desires, and the revolutionary deterioration of emotional connection. By often inspecting the nation of your marriage, you can discover and cope with troubles earlier than they become irreversible.

So, how can also want to you study the dominion of your marriage? Here are some critical steps to undergo in mind:

1. Communication: The basis of any pinnacle marriage is open and sincere verbal exchange. Spend time in conjunction with your companion and characteristic meaningful conversations approximately your dating. Listen carefully to their troubles, emotions, and goals, and respectfully communicate your perspectives and emotions. Strong verbal exchange can assist in figuring out regions for growth and making both occasions sense desired and understood.

Chapter 10: Identifying Signs Of Marital Issues

To avoid divorce in a wedding, it's miles critical to apprehend the signs and symptoms of marital troubles early on and to take proactive movements to deal with them. Couples who are aware of the ones signals can attempt to resolve their troubles and deliver a boost to their dating. Here are a number of the most fantastic caution indicators of marital troubles:

1. Communication breakdown: Misunderstandings, resentment, and dissatisfaction can end result from a lack of top communique in a marriage. If you and your accomplice are having problem expressing your feelings, listening actively, or having large conversations, this will be an indication that your marriage is in risk.

2. Constant squabbles: Frequent squabbles that grow rapid and are in no way truly resolved can suggest underlying marital issues. Conflict is an inevitable thing of any

courting; however on the equal time because it turns into too regularly, too strong, and too unresolved, it is able to harm the fabric of your marriage.

3. Emotional detachment: If you or your companion are emotionally separated and now not revel in related on an intimate or non-public level, your marriage may be in chance. Emotional detachment frequently results in feelings of loneliness and may have a damaging impact on commonplace happiness and pride inside the marriage.

4. Intimacy decline: A decline in emotional, bodily, or sexual intimacy may be an example of marital issues. When partners forestall being affectionate with each different, show little hobby in each distinct's lifestyles, or have a diminished desire for bodily intimacy, it's miles a sign that the emotional and bodily ties are deteriorating.

5. Trust problems: The basis of any ideal marriage is be given as authentic with. Trust problems can exist in case you or your partner

frequently distrust a further's terms or behavior, cover subjects, or have a information of infidelity. It is hard to expand a strong and lasting connection without don't forget.

6. Feeling unfulfilled or unhappy: When one or each events in a marriage revel in unfulfilled or unhappy, it is able to result in bitterness and discontent. This can be because of numerous factors, which consist of disappointed expectations, a loss of assist, or feeling trapped in an unwanted characteristic.

7. Ignoring each one-of-a-kind's desires: For a wedding to be healthful, every spouses ought to prioritize and address every other's emotional, physical, and intellectual requirements. When companions save you devoting time, attempt, and power to addressing the ones goals, emotions of overlook about and alienation can boom.

eight. Financial disagreements: Money is frequently a supply of competition in marriages. If you and your partner are frequently arguing approximately cash, have distinctive spending patterns, or are beneath massive financial hassle, it could be a demonstration of deeper troubles to your relationship.

9. Incompatibility: Divorce may additionally result whilst couples find out they have core disagreements about morals, ideologies, or aspirations in life that they are no longer able to art work thru.

10. Lack of Future Planning: It is a sign of a lack of determination to a dating if a pair isn't discussing their desires and aspirations or growing plans for the destiny together.

It's crucial to recollect that marriage is a complicated method, and recognizing those signs may not generally mean the stop of your marriage. However, spotting them early allows you to deal with the underlying troubles and are seeking expert help if crucial. Regular take a look at-ins, open and sincere communique, and a desire to paintings for your relationship will help you prevent divorce and create an first-rate and massive marriage.

Communication Breakdown and Conflict Resolution

Communication breakdown and struggle choice are two key elements of keeping a wedding wholesome and wealthy. Marriages can unexpectedly fall apart with out fantastic communique and the potential to handle disagreements peacefully. Couples want to consequently installation right communique talents and discover ways to negotiate arguments constructively.

Breakdowns in conversation can upward thrust up for a variety of reasons. When one or each companions war to express their emotions, dreams, or issues well, misunderstandings and frustration get up. Furthermore, terrible listening capabilities, a lack of empathy, and protective verbal exchange strategies should probably exacerbate the situation.

Couples can use quite a few techniques to avoid communication breakdowns. To begin, it's far critical to create an open and non-judgmental environment wherein each partners enjoy snug expressing themselves sincerely. Active listening, that is completely focusing at the speaker with out interrupting or growing responses in our heads, can also assist to sell well communique. Couples can also research empathy thru seeking to understand and validate each specific's emotions, despite the fact that they do not typically agree.

Another essential capacity for a satisfied marriage is struggle desire. Conflicts are unavoidable in any relationship, but how they may be resolved can have a massive impact on the marriage's ordinary properly-being. Unresolved confrontations can breed resentment, hostility, and a loss of agree with. Couples need to have a observe suitable struggle desire abilties to avoid divorce. This begins with spotting and addressing disputes as they stand up, in preference to permitting them to construct into massive issues. It is important to technique disagreements to discover a solution that advantages each occasions, in choice to trying to win or show oneself accurate.

Adopting a snug and courteous communication style is a beneficial conflict choice method. Couples can set up ground suggestions for dispute choice, which include fending off private attacks, talking certainly however civilly, and taking breaks even as feelings get overpowering.

Active listening is also vital in dispute preference. Each partner have to be allowed to hold their thing of view, at the identical time as the other listens closely and attempts to recognize theirs. This can useful resource within the buildup of empathy and the discount of defensiveness, making it easier to discover common floor.

Compromise and negotiation capabilities are also essential for struggle selection. Couples have to be open to trying new topics and developing with collectively beneficial answers. It is beneficial to brainstorm collectively and awareness on developing win-win results that do not overlook each spouses' desires and dreams.

Finally, couples who fail to speak efficiently or settle issues on their very very very own can advantage from receiving professional assist thru marriage counseling or treatment. A professional therapist can provide recommendation, teach precious skills, and beautify communication.

Evaluating Emotional Connection and Intimacy Levels.

Evaluating a marriage's emotional connection and intimacy ranges is essential for preserving a healthy and profitable dating. A robust emotional bond and closeness are essential in keeping a marriage together and preventing divorce.

First and maximum vital, emotional connection is the bedrock of a happy marriage. It involves being capable of recognize, aid, and empathize with one's accomplice. A loss of emotional connection regularly ends in emotions of abandonment, loneliness, and unhappiness. As a end result, assessing the emotional tie with one's spouse is crucial for figuring out the electricity of this connection. Couples should undergo in thoughts how properly they speak, how often they've got sizable talks, and whether or not or now not or not they enjoy emotionally supported through their companion.

Another essential aspect of a long-lasting marriage is physical and emotional intimacy. Physical intimacy encompasses affectionate touch, hugging, preserving palms, and preserving a physical connection in addition to sexual intimacy. In evaluation, emotional intimacy refers to sharing one's profound feelings, mind, and desires with one's partner. To installation emotional closeness, take delivery of as actual with, vulnerability, and open verbal exchange are required.

Chapter 11: Nurturing A Healthy Relationship

Building and fostering a strong connection is critical for stopping marriage and divorce. Maintaining a healthful and loving bond desires attempt, verbal exchange, empathy, and a choice to art work together to triumph over obstacles. Here are some critical matters to take to keep a healthy courting and keep away from divorce.

1 The ability to speak efficaciously is the cornerstone of any a achievement partnership. It is essential to brazenly and in reality percent one's perspectives, emotions, and problems. Effective conversation requires active listening, empathy, and the avoidance of protecting behavior. Checking in collectively along with your associate regularly and discussing any problems that get up can help prevent misunderstandings from developing into massive ones.

2. Spending high-quality time collectively is critical for retaining a robust emotional

connection. Spend time doing a little element you each experience, together with taking walks, looking movies, or in fact having a heartfelt chat. Making every one among a kind a concern and actually interested by a distinct's lives promotes a revel in of togetherness and enhances the link.

3. Trust and respect: A healthy partnership requires receive as right with and respect. Building and maintaining accept as true with desires honesty, dependability, and open communication. Respecting every distinct's thoughts, emotions, and barriers often gives a safe and loving environment. When agree with and understand are broken, it could bring about demanding situations and disputes within the partnership.

4. Conflict resolution abilities: While disagreements and conflicts are unavoidable in any dating, how they are dealt with may want to make a massive distinction. Practicing powerful conflict preference abilities, together with energetic listening,

compromise, and looking for on the identical time useful solutions, can assist to maintain minor disagreements from becoming large troubles. It is critical to approach confrontations frivolously and respectfully, with a focal point on locating answers instead of assigning blame.

5. Emotional resource: It is vital to offer emotional assist in your partner to preserve an outstanding dating. Being there for each other in appropriate and bad times generates a enjoy of comfort and reassurance. Validating one extra's emotions, lending a listening ear, and handing over comfort all contribute to a stronger emotional tie amongst companions.

6. Continual boom and self-improvement: Both partners want to artwork on private increase and self-development because of the reality that this contributes to the relationship's regular health. Regular self-mirrored image, intention placing, and achievement can inspire and inspire your

accomplice as nicely. Encourage each extraordinary's desires and offer help and encouragement along the manner.

Cultivating Effective Communication Skills

1. Active listening: This is one of the maximum essential components of right communication. This consists of giving remarks to demonstrate that you are actively listening, being gift and worried within the communication, and being privy to both verbal and nonverbal clues. This makes it less complicated to ensure that everyone feels understood and heard.

2. Make "I" statements: It's vital to make "I" statements in location of "you" statements at the same time as expressing your emotions or troubles. Expressing "You in no way spend enough time with me" can come seen as accusatory or blaming, while expressing "I enjoy neglected even as you spend an excessive amount of time at art work" encourages open and honest conversation.

three. Nonverbal conversation: Words by myself are not enough to maintain thoughts efficiently. Body language, tone of voice, and facial expressions are examples of non-verbal cues that often transmit more information than terms on my own. It's critical to recognize the ones cues and try and communicate your issue each orally and nonverbally.

4. Select the right time and vicinity: Effective verbal exchange is more likely to arise in the perfect environment. Select a time and region in which there may not be any disruptions or distractions and wherein every events can experience comfortable and calm. This creates a cushty and stress-free surroundings for sincere and open speak.

5. Develop empathy: Empathy is the capacity to realize and experience a few other character's emotions. You can enhance your comprehension and courting on the aspect of your accomplice through practicing empathy for your conversation. Give them your full

attention even as trying to recognize their element of view. This can contribute to the development of an environment of admire and understanding.

Rebuilding Trust and Creating a Safe Space.

1. Open and Honest Communication: Both spouses should be willing to speak brazenly and in fact with every specific to reestablish accept as true with and installation a steady location of their marriage. This involves speakme brazenly and truely approximately their dreams, desires, and worries as well as actively paying attention to preserve close to one another's viewpoints.

2. Set Boundaries: Establishing boundaries in a marriage is important to fostering a secure surroundings. Regarding conduct, communique, and personal place, each companions need to be aware about what's and isn't always suitable. Mutual recognize for every distinctive's limits promotes safety and recall.

3. Exercise Empathy and Understanding: Empathy and facts of each other's feelings and reports are important for repairing agree with among partners. This consists of accepting and validating every different's emotions, despite the fact that they will not coincide with one's point of view. Partners can installation a stable vicinity in which they every enjoy heard and supported via workout empathy.

4. Offer Apologies and Forgiveness: Both occasions have to be prepared to accept obligation for his or her errors and offer forgiveness to reestablish bear in mind. Sincere apologies ought to be provided, collectively with a pledge to alter or accurate the conduct that added at the take delivery of as authentic with to be violated. Likewise, forgiveness fortifies the basis of recall in marriage by way of way of the use of permitting every activities to move on and permit go of previous hurt.

5. Be Reliable and Dependable: Rebuilding be given as proper with calls for being dependable, regular, and able to maintaining pledges and agreements. Both events ought to show their dependability and trustworthiness through doing and speaking as promised.

6. Seek Professional Assistance: Seeking the advice of a therapist or counselor can be important at instances even as restoring recall in a marriage. Both partners can discover their feelings, deal with underlying troubles, and feature a observe powerful communique and agree with-building techniques in a steady and unbiased setting with the resource of in search of remedy.

7. Promote an Appreciation Culture: Establishing a steady surroundings in a wedding moreover entails regularly expressing love, thanks, and appreciation for every other. Building a super and provoking surroundings that promotes agree with and emotional safety is facilitated with the

resource of expressing gratitude for each other's efforts, tendencies, and contributions.

Reviving Emotional and Physical Intimacy.

1. Make verbal exchange a problem: Restoring emotional and physical intimacy calls for open and honest communication. Spend some time discussing your needs, wishes, and issues at the side of your partner. Pay near interest to how they may be feeling as well. This will lay a strong basis for reestablishing a connection.

2. Set aside time for each other: It's smooth to overlook spending superb time along side your associate the diverse every day rigors. Try your hardest to find out time on your schedule to interact in matters that you each love to do. Whether you spend time collectively on a date, go with the flow on a leisurely stroll, or certainly curl up on the couch, making time for each superb each day can foster a stronger emotional and bodily bond.

3. Express affection: Intimacy can be significantly restored thru small gestures of affection. Physical expressions of love, which encompass a heat hug, a passionate kiss, or a light contact, can assist re-ignite the hearth to your courting. Never undervalue the importance of bodily contact in fostering emotional closeness.

4. Try new sports activities as a pair: Trying new things together can be exciting and help re-light the excitement and freshness of your dating. Traveling to new locations, selecting up a hobby together, or experimenting inside the bed room are just a few examples of the way experiencing new matters together can re-light emotional and physical closeness.

five. Seek expert assist whilst critical: Don't be afraid to get expert assist if you and your accomplice are having problem reestablishing intimacy. Therapists or relationship counselors can offer direction and assist in resolving troubles with emotional and bodily closeness. They will let you in putting in place a steady environment for candid communicate and provide belongings to help you reestablish a near and effective bond.

6. Practice self-care: Restoring intimacy on your marriage calls for that you look after your private physical and intellectual health. Make sure to provide self-care sports that decrease pressure and foster positivity a top precedence. This can comprise doing bodily activity, operating in the direction of meditation, taking on a hobby, or starting off with encouraging friends and circle of relatives. You'll have more electricity and ability to dedicate yourself for your courting when you're in suitable physical and mental condition.

7. Have tolerance and information: It takes time, staying power, and work to rebuild emotional and physical connection. Recognize that there may be boundaries within the course and that change might not take area right away. To repair closeness, you want to be given and encourage one another on their

direction. Remain committed to the manner and renowned minor accomplishments, because the work you do will result in a much better and pleasurable relationship.

Chapter 12: Addressing Specific Marital Issues

Marriage is a lovable and holy union that calls for ongoing paintings, tolerance, and concession from each event. But marital problems can rise up frequently, causing strife and in all likelihood even the risk of divorce. Early detection and backbone of first-rate marital problems is critical to ensuring a robust and lengthy-lasting partnership and stopping the type of situation.

1. Ineffective Communication: One of the maximum everyday troubles in marriages is useless communication. Couples with inclined conversation skills often find out themselves in arguments, feeling not noted, or misinterpreted. Both occasions want to determine to honest and open conversation to clear up this problem. This calls for attentive listening, smooth communication of one's thoughts and feelings, and openness to the attitude of others. To beef up and fill in any gaps, you can moreover think about

getting professional assistance, which includes marriage counseling.

2. Issues with Trust: A strong and prolonged-lasting marriage is built on take into account. However, adultery, a loss of transparency between companions, or annoying critiques inside the past can all bring about keep in mind issues. It takes time, persistence, and continual paintings to rebuild receive as real with. It starts offevolved with every partners accepting obligation for his or her acts, speaking sincerely approximately their mind, and sharing worries. Complete honesty, openness, and a readiness to transport beyond hurts and bypass on are critical for keep in mind to be rebuilt.

3. Financial Disagreement: Money troubles can with out difficulty become a detail of contention and stress in a wedding. Conflict can surrender quit end result from disparate spending styles, unmet financial desires, or a loss of economic transparency. Open traces of conversation about coins are important for

couples to address financial concerns. Together, you need to create a rate variety, talk about your monetary desires, and determine what to spend and maintain. Financial unification and warfare avoidance can be fostered in marriages through open verbal exchange and regular check-ins.

four. Sexual Dissatisfaction: A satisfied and healthy marriage requires close to sexual touch. But sexual dissatisfaction also can forestall end result from troubles like mismatched libidos, loss of preference, or unsolved marital tensions. It is crucial to talk one's desires and desires in an open and nonjudgmental manner to address the ones demanding situations. Establishing a constant surroundings in which every couples feel relaxed talking about their expectations and searching into strategies to beautify their intercourse is crucial. Consulting a therapist or intercourse counselor can offer similarly route and assist in managing sexual troubles and improving intimacy.

five. Emotional Disconnect: Couples may have an emotional detachment from one another through the years. This can get up from no longer spending enough time collectively, ignoring emotional goals, or setting one of a kind responsibilities in advance of the relationship. Couples have to prioritize their dating and find time for each other to cope with emotional distance. Emotional connection can be rekindled via significant talks, not unusual date nights, and showing love and gratitude. Maintaining a strong and cohesive marriage requires that companions make an effort to apprehend and attend to each distinctive's emotional needs.

In precis, maintaining a glad and healthy marriage and stopping divorce rely upon addressing high-quality marital worries. A healthful prolonged-term dating requires open and sincere communication, don't forget-building, financial battle decision, stepped forward sexual pleasure, and fostering emotional connection.

Balancing Work and Personal Life.

Every human have to strike a stability amongst their personal and professional lives, and that is specially actual in relation to keeping a glad and healthful marriage. Striking a careful balance among one's commitments in the place of business and one's connections is important to preventing divorce.

To begin with, verbal exchange is critical to placing this equilibrium. Couples want to be sincere with each different approximately their expectancies, duties, and work schedules. Both partners can more effectively set up their time and make the crucial adjustments to meet every different's dreams if they're aware about a further's expert obligations. Honest talks approximately paintings-lifestyles balance and normal take a look at-ins can assist keep away from miscommunication and animosity from developing.

Setting limits is a few different vital detail. It's essential that human beings set barriers amongst their non-public and expert lives. This should consist of unique instances, like food or the weekends even as artwork-associated sports are prohibited. Couples can emphasize their relationships and spend super time together with the aid of setting those limitations. Setting limits moreover involves getting to know to refuse unreasonably excessive needs from the place of business that might intervene with personal time. It have to be important to location one's happiness first and to preserve a very good art work-existence balance.

Furthermore, hanging a stability amongst paintings and private existence requires powerful time control. Making a conscious strive to plot and prioritize your extracurricular sports will assist guarantee that your relationships aren't ignored. This is probably putting in place a shared calendar or installing region particular timeslots for family or entertainment activities the use of time manipulate software application software. People can avoid paintings taking up their private lives and keep a healthy paintings-existence stability thru handling their time properly.

Another important detail of maintaining a happy marriage is flexibility. When required, each companions need to be prepared to regulate and make concessions. This ought to entail reviewing work schedules or searching at one in every of a type art work arrangements that provide extra time for private or family sports activities. Being tolerant and inspiring of every extraordinary's expert desires and desires is a few different detail of pliability.

In addition, it is critical to consider self-care whilst aiming for a bit-lifestyles stability. Being completely present and worried in interpersonal relationships calls for looking after one's bodily and mental health. Every person should agenda time for fun and restorative hobbies, which include running out, taking up a interest, or putting out with buddies. People who prioritize self-care are higher capable of manipulate the rigors of the place of work without sacrificing their interpersonal connections.

In cease, preserving a healthy art work-lifestyles balance is important to keeping a marriage intact. Achieving this balance requires open communique, boundary-setting, powerful time manage, flexibility, and self-care, amongst various things. Couples can protect their marriage from the strain of an excessive amount of paintings via way of setting their relationships first and actively working to preserve an notable artwork-lifestyles balance. In the stop, keeping a healthy balance among paintings and private existence necessitates mutual records, flexibility, and self-discipline to the connection.

Managing Financial Strains and Differences.

A marriage's functionality to cope with financial troubles and disagreements is crucial to preventing divorce. One of the maximum crucial resources of pressure in a relationship may be cash, which regularly sparks disputes, animosity, and ultimately the dissolution of the union. However, couples can triumph over monetary troubles and pork up their dating with properly verbal exchange, compromise, and a nicely-concept-out plan.

When it involves managing financial constraints, open and sincere verbal exchange is important. Regular conversation about expectations, problems, and monetary dreams is important for couples. Being open and sincere approximately one's fee range, earnings, and spending styles is a part of this. Couples can better understand a extremely good's economic activities and collaborate to expand a strategy that works for absolutely everyone with the aid of having those discussions.

A price range that takes into consideration the economic constraints and disparities within the relationship is also vital. Financial desires which can be every quick- and prolonged-term, like emergency economic financial savings, debt reimbursement, and retirement making plans, have to be covered on this fee variety. Together, we are able to reduce monetary strain with the aid of manner of the usage of setting up a smooth spending and saving plan thru price range creation.

To control financial stresses and conflicts, compromise is likewise critical. Differing priorities and spending conduct amongst couples can motive friction. However, couples can benefit a harmonic economic balance by way of the use of compromising and finding a middle ground. This may want to entail setting policies on what can be spent freely, developing with progressive techniques to preserve coins, or reassessing your economic priorities.

When faced with excessive financial pressures, couples have to are attempting to find for professional help further to practising powerful communication and making compromises. Marital counselors and economic professionals can provide insightful advice and practical techniques for dealing with budget and settling disputes. These specialists can offer couples with intention steering and help in growing a technique to deal with their financial problems.

Couples should additionally stay understanding and galvanizing of each other even as they may be struggling financially. Emotionally charged subjects regarding coins can speedy increase into blame and animosity. Couples can create a optimistic environment to talk about and settle monetary disagreements with the resource of continuing to be understanding, affected character, and supportive of each other.

Couples should moreover hold in mind that monetary difficulties are a everyday trouble in most marriages and may be resolved.

Chapter 13: Dealing With Infidelity And Rebuilding Trust

One of the hardest and maximum emotionally taxing matters a associate can undergo is dealing with infidelity in their marriage. It is a betrayal and a lack of do not forget that rocks the relationship to its middle. However, couples can heal and stay married within the occasion that they've tenacity, willpower, and a common dedication to restoring recollect. In the way, go through in mind the following essential steps:

1. Address the emotional effects together: The partners ought to admit the harm, resentment, and grief added on thru the adultery. Establishing a regular environment that promotes candid and open conversation and we may additionally need to humans explicit their feelings without fear of repercussions is critical. Seek expert help or couples remedies that will help you have the ones difficult talks and make certain that each associate feels valued and heard.

2. Seek counseling: Infidelity commonly factors to deeper issues in a relationship that require attention. Couples counseling with a licensed therapist who can guide you through the headaches of infidelity are vital. Expert advice can offer independent views, encourage easy communication, and assist with growing plans for reestablishing bear in mind.

three. Reestablish recall: Following an affair, take delivery of as actual with need to be rebuilt, and this takes time and effort. The disloyal partner wishes to be prepared to private as an entire lot as their errors, explicit honest remorse, and make a determination to mending relationships. This might also moreover want to ivolve being honestly open and honest in all communications, disclosing mobile phone numbers or passwords, and taking obligation for his or her whereabouts. In addition, the betrayed associate need to set up limits and expectations with readability and be willing to don't forget the risk of rebuilding take into account.

four. Lay a sparkling foundation: Redefining the relationship is frequently crucial to rebuild a marriage after adultery. This want to ivolve assessing whether or not or no longer the expectations, values, and aspirations of the 2 companions are aligned by means of manner of going over them once more. It can also entail figuring out which unmet dreams or unsolved issues contributed to the adultery and cooperating to find out solutions.

five. It takes time to heal: Both in my view and as a pair, convalescing from infidelity calls for time. It's important to make room for processing the harm, mending emotionally, and regaining self esteem. This ought to entail going to man or woman remedy, taking care of oneself, and analyzing to forgive—every oneself and the dishonest associate.

6. Make a commitment to non-stop improvement: Maintaining a courting and preventing divorce necessitates a self-control to continuous development. Both companions should be organized to confront

their problems, use effective communique techniques, and take an energetic feature within the technique of recovery. This should encompass studying self-assist books, going to workshops, or getting greater counseling as wanted.

7. Put forgiveness into workout: Recovering from infidelity calls for forgiveness. It's crucial to consider that forgiveness is a method and will require a while. It way locating out to allow flow into of the bitterness and anger that might be preventing you from shifting on, not accepting or forgetting the adultery. It takes cooperation from each events to help the approach of forgiveness, that is a personal preference.

eight. Continue to speak overtly and in fact: Rebuilding be given as authentic with necessitates determination to honest and open communication. Both occasions want to be open and honest approximately their feelings, mind, and worries with out disturbing approximately criticism or reprisals. To make sure that every partners are on the equal net web web page and constantly striving within the course of a more healthy, more big dating, everyday test-ins and conversations regarding the fame of restoring agree with can help.

9. Accept effective modifications: An affair can feature a spark for superb transformation interior a wedding. It is probably a hazard for each partners to reevaluate their desires, reaffirm their self-discipline to every other, and make the desired changes to their man or woman and employer behaviors. Accept the hazard to boom, benefit facts, and make stronger your relationship thru mutual admire and information.

Although it could be difficult to regain be given as actual with after infidelity, it's miles feasible to save you divorce and create a stronger,

Are You Enjoying This Book? Do You Need A Book On How To Effectively Apologize to Your Loved Ones while at fault?

CLICK HERE TO GET HOW TO APOLOGIZE TO YOUR LOVED ONES

5. Resolving Resentment and Rebuilding Emotional Connection.

In a wedding, resentment can be a poisonous feeling that grade by grade erodes the emotional bond a number of the companions. It is a response that takes location whilst one associate believes the opportunity has wronged them and motives them to revel in indignant or sour. Resentment can in the end purpose a breakdown in communication, distance, and divorce if it is not remedied. Couples can, however, recover from animosity and decorate their dating inside the occasion that they have the essential time, knowledge, and electricity of mind to mending the emotional rift.

Acknowledging and taking duty for your damage or anger is the first step inside the direction of overcoming resentment. Without setting blame or passing judgment, each events must be inclined to speak their feelings really and freely. It is vital to preserve in thoughts that emotions are real and appropriate and that it's miles important to discover about and realise the studies and viewpoints of every partners.

Next, supply each different some time to actively listen to each other. This is making an attempt to understand the underlying desires and feelings being said further to in fact hearing what's being stated. Reaffirm on your partner which you are aware of their emotions and which you recognize their attitude.

Accepting responsibility for one's deeds and behaviors that might have fueled animosity is critical. To discover any styles or behaviors that would have irritated or invalidated your accomplice, you need to have interaction in introspection and self-reflected picture. Express regret to your preceding behavior and pledge honestly to do better.

Empathy and compassion education are also crucial for reestablishing emotional connection. Try to understand your associate's wishes, stressful conditions, and tales with the useful resource of putting yourself in their feature. Acknowledge their emotions and growth help to demonstrate empathy. This can assist every spouses enjoy cushty expressing themselves and resolving their differences in a sincere surroundings.

Getting expert assist can also be crucial at the same time as strolling with resentment. Therapists or marriage counselors can provide direction and assist couples speak. They can help couples in figuring out the underlying reasons for their conflicts and offer techniques and strategies for productively resolving them.

Maintaining the connection actively is every different trouble of restoring emotional connection. Prioritize spending high-quality time together and find time for every unique. Take part in a laugh sports activities sports together and make new reminiscences. Recognize your partner's efforts and accomplishments and precise your gratitude. Little acts of compassion and love should make a massive difference in assisting spouses mend their emotional dating.

And ultimately, the essential issue to finishing resentment is forgiveness. Letting pass of bitterness and fury is what forgiveness consists of, no longer forgetting or accepting merciless deeds. It's a hard technique that requires time. Recognize that forgiving someone is about your emotional fitness, no longer about the alternative person. Resentment can be allow move of, facilitating healing and joint ahead motion for the 2 events.

Patience, know-how, and a determination to private development are important for resolving anger and restoring emotional connection in a married courting. Both partners must receive duty for his or her emotions, actively pay attention, and interact in acts of compassion and expertise. Getting expert assist might also assist recover from the ones traumatic situations. Couples can triumph over animosity and guide their emotional tie through taking care of every special, expressing gratitude, and forgiving one another. This can ultimately save you divorce and bring about a happier and better marriage.

Embracing Compromise and Forgiveness.

Any marriage want to include compromise because it consists of setting a balance some of the wishes, desires, and viewpoints of the 2 events involved. It necessitates open communique, attentive listening, and a readiness to study one among a type elements of view. Couples can prevent strength clashes and installation a peaceful environment wherein each activities revel in desired and understood thru the usage of accepting compromise.

In contrast, forgiveness is important to the approach of recovery and receive as proper with-building following disagreements or mistakes. It involves choosing to move ahead with comprehension, empathy, and compassion as opposed to keeping onto grudges, wrath, and the desire for vengeance. Couples can heal from past hurts, deepen their dating, and lay the muse for future improvement and take delivery of as actual with thru forgiving each other.

Accepting forgiveness and making concessions circulate hand in hand. Couples who're inclined to make concessions are more likely to exercise variations and gain perception from every different's viewpoints. Furthermore, it's miles less difficult to allow pass of the past and create place for perception and improvement on the same time as forgiveness is gift.

Certain strategies can be used to assist a marriage embody forgiveness and compromise. The most crucial detail is to talk efficiently. Speaking honestly and overtly, couples want to actively take notice of every distinct while furthermore speaking their want and dreams. This lets in a deeper comprehension of each other's viewpoints, which allows the invention of solutions that please all aspects.

Empathy education is a in addition tactic. You could possibly find out not unusual floor through acknowledging and accepting your accomplice's emotions and opinions. It demonstrates a readiness to recall subjects from their issue of view, encouraging communication and cooperation.

Furthermore, the improvement of a robust and judgment-loose surroundings is essential for the achievement of forgiving. Fostering frank communique and transparency permits every sports to make an apology, apologize, and try to reestablish believe.

Finally, it's far essential to interact in self-assessment and personal development. Forgiveness can come greater with out issue even as we take transport of obligation for our acts and broadly recognized our flaws. In our marriage, we're better capable of offer and acquire forgiveness and compromise at the same time as we constantly art work on ourselves.

To sum up, accepting forgiveness and compromise is vital to preventing divorce and maintaining a satisfied, exciting marriage. Couples can clear up disagreements, beef up their relationship, and construct a committed and long-lasting connection via actively engaging in effective communique, empathy, strong environment creation, and private development.

6. Strengthening Your Marriage for the Long Term.

Marriage is a holy bond shaped through way of human beings who have selected to percentage their lives, pleasures, and traumatic situations. However, if a wedding isn't properly maintained and cared for, its basis might probably go to pot with time. Let's test a few techniques for you to help to boost the wedding inside the long time.

1. Effective Communication: Communication is the muse of any healthy dating. Strong couples recognize the value of open, honest, and nonjudgmental communique. The need for energetic listening, expressing feelings well, and discussing issues without blame or defensiveness is emphasised at a few degree inside the ebook. Couples can create a strong region for open communicate, enhance know-how, and settle disagreements constructively via manner of honing those capabilities.

2. Emotional Connection: Emotional connection is crucial in a long-term partnership. The ebook emphasizes the need to constantly particular love, admiration, and useful useful resource. Small moves together with expressing "I love you," giving reward, or surely spending excellent time collectively can assist to enhance the emotional bond among spouses. The ebook moreover advises couples to prioritize emotional goals, studies every different's love languages, and have interaction in sports activities that increase emotional intimacy frequently.

3. Mutual Respect and Trust: The cornerstones of a sturdy and healthy marriage are mutual apprehend and acquire as actual with. The ebook emphasizes the need to address one another with kindness, empathy, and information. It encourages couples to understand each exceptional's limits, values, and area of expertise. Building trust involves being dependable, honest, and apparent in all facets of the relationship. Couples can create a secure and regular environment in which each companions sense valued and preferred with the resource of fostering admire and keep in mind.

four. Nurture Friendships: Friendships are the inspiration of prolonged-time period partnerships. The necessity of nurturing the friendship problem of marriage is emphasized within the e-book via carrying out comparable pursuits, interests, and sports. Couples are recommended to prioritize high-quality time together, laughter, and enjoyment. Couples can enhance their bond and revel in each different's business enterprise as they grow antique by way of the use of the usage of cultivating their friendship.

five. Personal Growth and Development: The book emphasizes the importance of private boom and development in a happy marriage. It encourages companions to guide each precise's hopes, dreams, and personal dreams. Couples can add new ideas, enthusiasm, and depth to their courting through the usage of continuously growing and growing as human beings. The book recommends that couples do new subjects collectively, have a observe from every different, and project themselves to keep evolving as a partnership.

6. Seek Professional Help: Despite our excellent efforts, couples frequently come across seemingly insurmountable boundaries. In such instances, the book concedes that obtaining expert assist might be effective. Marriage counselors or courting experts can provide particular advice, resources, and strategies. They can help couples in navigating

hard situations, improving verbal exchange, and strengthening their bond.

To summarize, extended-time period marital strengthening consists of conscious paintings, determination, and a willingness to have interaction inside the courting. The ebook "How to Save Your Marriage" gives crucial insights and practices that could help couples in laying a business enterprise basis, improving verbal exchange, preserving emotional connection, and cultivating mutual respect and be given as real with. Couples can boom an extended-lasting, giant, and joyous relationship with the resource of implementing the ones strategies and walking on their relationship frequently.

Chapter 14: Building A Shared Vision And Goals

Creating a commonplace imaginative and prescient and desires in a wedding is critical for a superb and enduring connection.

Couples need to have regular conversations about their prolonged-term dreams and goals to begin organizing a commonplace vision. This includes speaking approximately critical subjects which includes technique dreams; own family making plans, monetary safety, and personal improvement. Couples can assemble a strong foundation for his or her courting via the use of expressing their separate visions and uniting them proper into a unmarried imaginative and prescient.

When putting desires, it's far essential to make sure that they're practical, measurable, and functionality. Both partners must enjoy ownership and determination to those targets, that could boom a feel of shared duty and teamwork. Setting timelines and dreams can also resource in tracking improvement and provoking.

Couples want to prioritize tremendous conversation inside the pursuit of a commonplace imaginative and prescient and desires. This is actively being attentive to each other, sharing one's emotions and problems, and finding commonplace floor. When disagreements emerge, it's miles crucial to cope with them rapid and create solutions that fulfill the goals of every partners.

Creating a unified vision and dreams moreover necessitates persistent examination and adjustment. As human beings enlarge and situations change, it is essential to revisit and think over again the not unusual vision and desires often. This will help to make sure that they remain modern-day and constitute the couple's converting needs and objectives.

Building a shared vision and desires takes time, staying electricity, information, and compromise. Couples have to famend that they'll be humans with distinct reviews and that finding not unusual floor can take time and effort. Couples, but, can build a basis of keep in mind and togetherness thru prioritizing open and honest communication, enhancing the hazard of preserving off divorce.

Finally, growing a common imaginative and prescient and desires in a marriage is vital for preserving off divorce. Couples can construct a cohesive imaginative and prescient that shows their shared values and dreams by manner of actively discussing and mixing their separate perspectives. Setting practical and measurable goals, prioritizing powerful communication, and reading and updating the shared vision and goals often are all crucial components of a extraordinary and satisfactory marriage. Couples can nourish their connection and raise the opportunity of a protracted and pleasurable marriage by using way of way of walking together as a group.

Fostering Mutual Respect and Appreciation.

Mutual respect and admiration are essential for the fulfillment and durability of a marriage. When companions respect and recognize one another, they devise a nice environment wherein love and statistics can flourish.

Couples must cope with every distinctive with love, records, and task to create mutual apprehend. This includes actively listening to each other, respecting every specific's viewpoints, and refraining from disrespectful behavior which includes demeaning or dismissive remarks. Respecting each precise's obstacles and private place is also vital, permitting every associate to hold their independence and individuality inside the partnership.

Appreciation is crucial in putting in a strong foundation of love and gratitude in a marriage. Expressing gratitude for every special's efforts, sacrifices, and developments fosters high quality emotions and a enjoy of properly well really worth in the partnership.

Small actions of appreciation, together with verbal reputation, expressing gratitude, or performing some aspect special for your accomplice, can help sell reciprocal appreciation.

Couples should workout extraordinary conversation to gather a manner of existence of recognize and admiration. Active listening, seeking information, and keeping off defensive behavior are all a part of this. It is essential to address confrontations with dignity and empathy, concentrated on answers as opposed to assigning blame.

Couples can also cultivate mutual understand and admiration thru way of actively making an investment of their relationship. Making time for each distinct, collaborating in common sports, and showing hobby in each distinct's lives are all part of this. It is also essential to recognize and apprehend each different's accomplishments and milestones, no matter how massive or small.

Overall, cultivating mutual admire and appreciation in a marriage entails chronic attempt and power of thoughts at the a part of every spouses. It necessitates open and honest communication, empathy, and a dedication to prioritize your partner's well-being and happiness. You can construct a strong and exceptional marriage with the resource of fostering these characteristics for your marriage.

Practicing Self-Care and Individual Growth.

Self-care and person boom in a marriage are vital for every spouses' popular fitness and happiness. While marriage is a partnership, it is in addition vital to apprehend that each character within the marriage has their personal set of wishes, desires, and private improvement path. Building a strong revel in of self and pursuing personal development can improve the connection and bring new levels of satisfaction to each partners.

Prioritizing one's very personal physical, emotional, and intellectual properly-being is an crucial element of running towards self-care in a wedding. This includes taking care of oneself thru normal workout, nutritious vitamins, pinnacle sufficient sleep, and strain control. It moreover includes looking after one's very own emotional desires with the useful resource of accomplishing exciting sports, practising self-compassion, and getting help from cherished ones or professionals at the same time as important.

Individual boom, in addition to physical and emotional self-care, is vital for private improvement inside a marriage. Pursuing hobbies and pursuits that provide achievement and strain personal boom, which include studying a new potential or growing a innovative outlet, may be part of this. It may include accomplishing self-meditated photo and personal development paintings, alongside aspect remedy or training, to higher recognize oneself and art work via any private issues or proscribing beliefs.

While that specialize in man or woman increase internal a partnership can also seem contradictory, it's miles critical to recognise that a robust experience of self can gain the wedding. When each partners are actively operating on non-public improvement, the relationship profits a experience of success, self assure, and self-cognizance. This can result in superior communique, greater know-how, and a higher bond amongst partners.

Respecting each one-of-a-type's limits and developing room for every exceptional to pursue their pastimes and passions is likewise a part of schooling self-care and character boom in a wedding. Rather than trying to persuade or manipulate every distinctive's objectives and goals, it's miles critical to guide and sell them. Couples can gather a harmonic balance among private development and shared critiques via way of nurturing every great's development.

When it entails workout self-care and character growth in a marriage, conversation is crucial. It is essential for each couples to share their private wishes, aspirations, and goals freely. Setting limits around personal time and space, further to building conduct and rituals that encourage person boom, can all contribute to this. Check-ins frequently and frank conversations regarding private development may also need to make each companions feel heard, understood, and supported.

Finally, it's far important to realize and widely diagnosed every specific's personal boom triumphs, and achievements. Couples can create a pleasant and inspiring environment for person increase with the useful resource of being every one-of-a-kind's cheerleaders. This can include commemorating achievements, handing over terms of encouragement, or even cheerleading inside the route of tough times. Recognizing and respecting every specific's efforts in the direction of non-public development can give a boost to the wedding's experience of collaboration and mutual help.

Practicing self-care and individual growth in a marriage is crucial for each spouses' massive nicely-being and pleasure. Couples can lay a stable foundation for a fulfilling and thriving courting via emphasizing non-public dreams, pursuing character increase, and provoking open communication and manual. Remember that a happy, fulfilled individual outcomes in a happier, more first-class marriage.

7. Tools and Resources for Marriage Transformation.

Couples can use plenty of techniques and offerings to help them on their manner to a wholesome and satisfying marriage. These equipment can offer path, insights, and realistic strategies for enhancing conversation, resolving problems, and strengthening bonds.

Marriage counseling is a famous method for marriage transformation. Marriage counselors are certified specialists who offer a safe and supportive environment for couples to speak about their problems and discover answers. Counselors help couples in figuring out volatile behaviors, improving communication, and developing conflict choice techniques thru individual and couples remedy intervals.

Couples workshops or retreats are a few other exceptional useful resource for marriage alternate. These extensive durations allow couples to walk a long way from their normal physical games and listen certainly on their love. Workshops on problems together with verbal exchange, intimacy, and warfare selection frequently include interactive sports activities, organisation discussions, and expert-led talks. Couples seminars will help you get perception into your relationship and study new abilities to help you set up a stronger marriage.

Books and on-line property also are beneficial for transforming a wedding. Books created through marriage and courting professionals can offer treasured insights, recommendation, and realistic tactics for boosting your marriage. "The Seven Principles for Making Marriage Work" by manner of way of John Gottman, "Hold Me Tight" via Sue Johnson, and "The Five Love Languages" with the aid of way of Gary Chapman are 3 distinguished books about marriage transformation. These books have provided many viewpoints on marriage further to mind for growing a strong and thriving courting.

Online assets which includes blogs, podcasts, and marriage and relationship web web sites can also be useful equipment for marriage reform. These web sites frequently offer articles, movies, and expert interviews on a large form of problems, collectively with communication, battle resolution, and intimacy. Online device are available at any time, making them perfect for couples who choose to art work on their marriage at their personal pace.

Aside from professional gear and property, community-primarily based tasks and guide companies can help with marriage transition.

These applications often provide a sturdy and beneficial environment for couples to hook up with others who are dealing with comparable problems. Couples can proportion their reviews, examine from others, and looking for encouragement and help from friends who've had comparable demanding situations.

Couples who preference to adjust their marriage have many techniques and sources at their disposal. Couples have numerous alternatives for acquiring the recommendation of a marriage counselor, attending a couples workshop, reading books, gaining access to on-line belongings, or becoming a member of a assist organisation. Couples ought to discover tools and services that communicate to them and meet their person goals and aspirations. Couples can redecorate their marriage and increase a sturdy and wholesome relationship that lasts a lifetime with devotion, attempt, and the remarkable equipment.

Effective Communication Exercises.

Communication is essential in each courting, however it's far more essential in marriage. Couples who talk effectively experience higher relationships, more with out issues settle disagreements, and assemble a deeper facts and reference to every different. Communication abilties, as a substitute, are not usually innate and may be acquired and more suited with exercise. Here are a few sensible verbal exchange sports sports that couples can do to decorate marital communique.

1. Active Listening: Active listening is a way that calls as a way to actually have interaction together together with your companion while they're speakme. Giving them your whole attention, retaining eye touch, and that specialize in understanding their issue of view in vicinity of planning your response are all important. Active listening can be practiced via couples with the aid of manner of taking turns speakme approximately a certain situation be counted at the same time as the opportunity partner listens cautiously. After

that, opposite roles and contemplate on what your companion stated to reveal which you were listening.

2. Reflective Feedback: Reflective feedback is a technique that consists of restating and summarizing what the alternative person stated to ensure right comprehension. This activity improves clarity, decreases misconceptions, and promotes open and sincere conversation. Partners can percent their perspectives or feelings in turn, after which the listener can rephrase what they heard to ensure they understood effectively. This lets in any misinterpretations to be addressed and remedied, further to demonstrating which you regard and recognize your accomplice's issue of view.

three. Nonverbal Communication: Nonverbal communique can be very critical in marital verbal exchange. Body language, facial expressions, tone of voice, and gestures are all examples of nonverbal communication. Couples can workout nonverbal verbal exchange bodily video games through manner of collaborating in sports activities that require them to speak thru nonverbal clues. Partners, as an instance, can take turns blindfolding and instructing each exclusive, depending solely on nonverbal clues to direct their sports. This hobby allows couples come to be greater aware about nonverbal clues and encourages them to talk more efficaciously through them.

four. Awareness of Timing and Tone: Timing and tone are vital elements of powerful communique. Couples can do bodily video video games to end up more aware about their communique timing and tone. For example, partners can act out conditions in which one associate is the speaker and the opposite is the listener. The speaker can exercise turning in their message the use of severa tones and timing whilst the listener presents comments on how the ones additives have an impact on the general communication. This interest teaches couples how their tone and timing have an effect on their message and the manner to change those additives for advanced conversation.

five. Conflict Resolution: The motive of this hobby is to resolve troubles productively and in a well mannered way. Couples can paintings on a selected hassle or struggle of words through taking turns expressing their perspectives and feelings. The goal is to attain a on the equal time applicable solution that considers every companions' needs and dreams. It is important to actively concentrate to each other, validate every specific's emotions, and avoid judgment or defensiveness.

6. Weekly Check-In: Schedule a check-in conversation as quick as each week to discover how every partner is feeling, any issues or troubles they will have, and any potential changes desired in your courting. This exercising encourages normal conversation, permitting partners to live in touch and control problems earlier than they end up excessive.

7. Appreciation and Gratitude: In this interest, people specific their appreciation and gratitude for every distinct's efforts, assist, and affection. Take turns sharing precise matters you need approximately each distinctive and expressing thanks for the best developments or behaviors that contribute to the electricity of your courting. This interest promotes an terrific and worrying surroundings on the same time as emphasizing the want of appreciating and valuing every other.

Remember that powerful communique is a capabilities that takes time and effort to comprehend. Couples who participate in those physical sports often can enhance their conversation abilties, advantage a better statistics of each specific, and set up a stronger and extra glad marriage.

Chapter 15: Relationship-Building Activities

Relationship-constructing sports and date mind are vital to preserving the spark in a relationship. Whether you're in a new dating or had been collectively for years, sporting out thrilling and substantial sports activities regularly can assist to reinforce your bond and create lasting memories.

1. Enroll in a cooking splendor collectively: Learning to put together a new delicacies together can be a fun and concerned manner to bond. You'll actually have a great lunch to look in advance to in some time.

2. Volunteer together: Choose a motive this is crucial to every of you and spend an afternoon giving decrease returned to the community. Not only will you be growing a difference, but you may additionally be strengthening your bonds with the resource of working collectively closer to a commonplace goal.

3. Go on a walk or a nature walk: Being outside can be quite invigorating and rejuvenating. Exploring a modern day route or park collectively along with your pals lets you hook up with nature whilst additionally connecting.

four. Plan a marvel date: Plan a considerate nighttime to your sweetheart. A romantic candlelit dinner at domestic, a picnic inside the park, or tickets to a concert they've got been longing to wait are all opportunities. The detail of wonder affords delight and demonstrates your trouble to your partner.

five. Make a scrapbook or picture album: Put collectively a scrapbook or picture album of your pleasant recollections and snap shots. You'll be reminded of all the memorable events you've got were given shared as you preserve in thoughts and placed the pages together. This exercising now not remarkable strengthens your relationship but additionally permits you to make a souvenir that you may experience for years to come.

6. Host a recreation night time time: Whether you enjoy board games, card video games, or video games, a sport night time time may be a super possibility to engage at the same time as furthermore task some best contention. You can also need to even invite different couples to enroll in you on a double date and flip it into a communal hobby.

7. Plan a weekend journey: Plan a weekend getaway to a vacation spot you every preference to go to. It should now not want to be a long way or pricey; genuinely changing surroundings and devoting time to each special can do wonders on your relationship.

eight. Have a movie marathon: Choose a subject or a series of films that each of you enjoy and spend a quiet middle of the night at the sofa. Make a few popcorn, munchies, and liquids for the suitable movie night.

nine. Exercise collectively: Exercising collectively now not best maintains you each healthful, but it also permits you to have amusing and bond. Take a run, a dance beauty, or a new gymnasium elegance together. Endorphins launched at some stage in workout also can enhance your mood and create an first-rate surroundings.

10. Plan a do-it-your self undertaking: Working on a do-it-yourself challenge together can be a amusing manner to collaborate and bring a few element vital. Working collectively on a undertaking, whether or not it is making fixtures, painting a room, or setting up a lawn, maybe a nice enjoy.

eleven. Host a spa night time time in your personal residence, entire with scented candles, calming music, and massages. Take turns pampering every different and spend some valuable time interesting together.

12. Attend a workshop or beauty: Sign up for a workshop or magnificence that each of you are inquisitive about. A portray elegance, a dance workshop, or a cookery demonstration are all opportunities. Learning a few component new in conjunction with your

buddies can be a fun and enriching experience.

Remember that the critical thing up to now thoughts and dating-building sports is to popularity on exceptional time and proper connection. You can construct your friendships and create lasting recollections through taking thing in sports activities which you both revel in and could let you increase together.

Chapter 16: Understanding Why Your Marriage Is Failing

Identify the commonplace reasons and signs of a failing marriage

When a marriage is dangerous, miserable, and unsatisfying for each activity, it is failing. A failing marriage will have loads of reasons and symptoms and signs and symptoms, but some of the maximum preferred ones are as follows:

A loss of connection and communiqué: A happy and healthful marriage is based upon on connection and verbal exchange. Couples lose the emotional closeness and link that binds them together after they prevent talking, comprehending, and taking note of one another. They may enjoy isolation, loneliness, and misunderstandings within the partnership.

Constant disdain and complaint: These are toxic attitudes that undermine accept as real with and appreciate in a wedding. Couples who're often berating, blaming, and insulting each other foster a adverse, toxic environment that makes it difficult to artwork through issues and settle conflicts. They can also moreover additionally harbor animosity, rage, and harm toward every different.

Loss of intimacy and affection: A satisfied and pleasant marriage relies upon on intimacy and affection. Couples can also enjoy reduce off from every other when they not have the identical stage of physical and sexual desire and connection. In the connection, they will moreover sense rejected, unloved, and unwelcome.

Infidelity and betrayal: These are grave transgressions of a married couple's dedication and loyalty. The believe and security that shape the idea of a wedding are harmed whilst one or both partners lie, cheat, or withhold records from one another. In addition, they'll revel in emotions of hurt, betrayal, and devastation because of their accomplice's behavior, similarly to guilt, disgrace, and regret for their very personal.

Disagreements and conflicts: These are unavoidable and regular in any relationship, but if they'll be not controlled nicely, they're capable to show unfavourable and bad. Couples that argue hundreds, deeply, and ineffectively purpose a superb deal of strain and strain of their marriage. In addition, they will revel in frustration, discontent, and sadness in the partnership.

Analyze your own state of affairs and the unique troubles to your relationship

You need to first understand the problems on your marriage and their causes if you want to store it. Regarding your non-public occasions and the precise problems which you and your associate are handling, you need to be frank and impartial. You must be inclined to confront the reality and pose a few difficult inquiries to yourself.

You can ask yourself the following queries, for instance:

What are the primary points of competition or war of words among you and your partner?

How frequently do you fight or argue over the ones disagreements?

How does it make you enjoy to combat or argue along side your partner?

How do you deal with and settle these disputes or troubles?

How do those troubles or disagreements effect your happiness and your relationship?

What feature do you play in the ones disputes or issues?

What do you need and need out of your companion in your marriage?

Are your needs and expectancies suitable and practical?

Are your partner and your marriage assembly your goals and expectations?

How do you talk in your associate your desires and expectations?

How do you react to the needs and expectations of your companion?

What are your dating's advantages and downsides?

What traits of your courting are right and horrible?

What characteristics of your companion and your marriage do you locate endearing and valuable?

What elements of your accomplice and your marriage trouble you and make you indignant?

How do you express your gratitude and affection in your accomplice?

How do you control your distaste and bitterness toward your accomplice?

To what quantity are you devoted in your accomplice and your matrimony?

To what quantity are you committed and devoted to your partner and your marriage?

How are you able to assist and uplift your associate and your union?

In what strategies do you honor and remember in your companion and your union?

How do you experience yourself, your companion, and your marriage?

How do you amplify and examine for your marriage and with your accomplice?

How do you strike a stability amongst your accomplice, your own family, your approach, and yourself in terms of time and electricity?

How do you appearance after your health and well-being?

You could have a extra profound and lucid comprehension of your non-public activities and the proper troubles in your relationship via responding to the ones questions. Additionally, you may pinpoint the matters that require artwork and the steps you want to do to maintain your marriage intact.

Evaluate your companion's mindset and feelings

Being capable of recognize and honor your companion's angle and emotions is important to a strong and pleased marriage. It's relevant in case your partner views and studies the world in some different way from you.

As a depend of reality, it may make a contribution to the depth and kind of your partnership. But in case you do not take the time to understand them, it may additionally bring about miscommunications, disputes, and animosity.

You need to have interaction in empathy-building and active listening if you are to evaluate your partner's factor of view and emotions. The functionality to region oneself in every different character's characteristic and revel in their feelings is called empathy. The capability to pay interest carefully, observe up with inquiries, and repeat decrease lower returned what you concentrate is called energetic listening.

The following levels will help you in assessing your spouse's angle and feelings:

Request that your accomplice speak to you about their feelings and mind. Encourage them to speak actually and freely with out worrying approximately backlash or condemnation. Show them that you are interested in their evaluations and feelings.

Pay near interest to your companion and cope with them with understand. Refrain from arguing, interrupting, or supplying recommendation. Pay hobby to what they have got to mention in choice to what you need to mention. Pay interest to their facial expressions, tone of speech, and frame language. Consider the which means underlying their statements.

In your very personal phrases, repeat what you have heard. To display off your interest and ensure you recognise what your partner is saying, attempt paraphrasing what they're pronouncing. Saying "So what you are saying is..." or "If I understand you efficiently, you experience..." are examples of what you may say.

Respect and validate your associate's attitude and feelings. Even if you disagree with them, well known and recognize their feelings and component of view. You can also reply with, "I can see why you suspect that way..." in addition to "I can don't forget the way you revel in..." Don't downplay, bargain, or push aside their factor of view or emotions.

Feel compassion on your accomplice. Attempt to enjoy their feelings and have a have a look at the arena from their point of view. You may additionally respond with, "I apprehend the manner you revel in..." or perhaps "I could experience the identical manner if I had been in your scenario..." Avoid contrasting, contradicting, or evaluating their angle and emotions.

To elucidate and examine their point of view and feelings, use open-ended inquiries. Express interest and interest about their emotions and mindset. You may additionally moreover reply with, "Can you inform me extra about that?" or perhaps "How did that make you enjoy?" Never query, reproach, or area the blame for their factor of view and emotions on them.

Tell your accomplice how plenty you admire and assist them. I apprehend their sharing their mind and feelings with you.

Tell them you recognize and cherish their evaluations and emotions. You might also respond with, "I admire you organising as an lousy lot as me..." similarly to "I am right here for you..." Never belittle, condemn, or lecture someone for their point of view or emotions.

These suggestions permit you to have a look at your accomplice's point of view and emotions in a civil and beneficial way. Additionally, you may beef up your marriage and enhance your relationship and communique collectively along side your associate. Recall that each your element of view and your companion's feelings are valid and tremendous.

Acknowledge your feature and duty in the situation

Taking obligation on your issue inside the trouble and owning up in your errors is one of the toughest however maximum crucial ranges to saving your marriage. You can not deny or excuse your very very own mistakes, nor are you capable of hold your accomplice liable for the whole lot that went incorrect. It is critical that you well known the repercussions of your actions and how they have got impacted your partner and your relationship.

You should take the subsequent movements as a way to take delivery of your part within the circumstance and your duty:

Own up in your shortcomings. When discussing the movements or inactions that you took that contributed to the troubles in your marriage, be honest and awesome. You may say, as an instance, "I admit that I grow to be selfish and not noted your desires..." in addition to "I admit that I modified into disrespectful and hurtful to you..."

Admit your regret and remorse. Express your heartfelt remorse for the subjects you probably did and the damage they precipitated for your accomplice and your union. You may say, for example, "I am deeply sorry for what I did and how I made you feel..." or maybe "I regret that I induced you so much pain and harm..."

Make an apology and request a reconciliation. Ask for your companion's pardon and desire to place in the attempt to restore the relationship. You can also moreover say, for instance, "I ask for your forgiveness and preference that you could deliver me each different danger..." or maybe "I need to reconcile with you and rebuild our consider and love..."

Make reparations and amends. Show that you are committed to improving every your courting and your actions. This can be presenting an apology, growing with a plan to behave better, or performing some thing to undo the harm that become done1. You might also say, as an example, "I will do something it takes to make subjects right with you..." and "I could have a study thru with the moves we agreed directly to recuperation our problems..."

You are demonstrating to your spouse your humility, obligation, and willingness to enhance thru accepting your detail in the hassle and your obligation. Additionally, you're permitting your marriage to be healed, forgiven, and restored.

Determine your goals and expectations for the wedding

Determining your expectations and desires for the wedding is one of the maximum essential components to saving your marriage. What form of marriage you choice and the way you want to get there want to be certainly and together understood by way of way of the usage of you and your partner. Your individual and couple goals need to be in keeping with every unique and be applicable and practical.

You want to perform the subsequent on the way to verify your expectations and dreams for the wedding:

Talk approximately your morals and thoughts. Respect and information of one another's values and ideals, in addition to how they have an impact in your expectancies and aspirations for the marriage, are critical for you and your associate. You could in all likelihood preserve brilliant reviews about sex, parenting, coins, or religion, as an example. On those subjects, you need to come to a compromise or agree to vary without passing judgment or criticizing each specific.

Determine your want and goals. It is critical for you and your associate to speak and receive a distinct's want and dreams, similarly to how they impact your expectations and aspirations for the union. You may, for example, have high-quality dreams and picks in phrases of closeness, affection, communique, or resource. In order to keep away from ignoring or undervaluing every different, you have to strive your wonderful to residence each other's wants and needs, or compromise and supply them priority.

Establish measurable, unique objectives. Setting smooth, quantifiable dreams in your marriage and figuring out the way to get there need to be finished by means of you and your companion. You can also moreover need to paintings on developing your intimacy, believe, conversation, connection, or struggle decision talents, for example. You should make clear what those dreams advise to you, how you could music your development, and the stairs you will take to get there.

Go over and replace your objectives and expectations. Regularly reviewing and revising your expectancies and dreams for the marriage, further on your improvement inside the route of them, is critical for you and your companion. For instance, you may probable need to modify your goals and necessities in light of evolving possibilities, problems, or conditions. It's crucial to widely diagnose your successes, draw education out of your errors, and preserve to paintings within the route of your shared dreams.

Chapter 17: Taking Action To Save Your Marriage

Explain the concept and benefits of unilateral motion

When you behave unilaterally, it manner that you achieve this independently of your associate and without relying on their guide or approval The foundation of unilateral conduct is the belief that you can enhance your marriage thru way of changing yourself, in area of seeking to trade your associate. The concept that you are in fee of your private happiness, health, and conduct no matter what your companion does is also the foundation of unilateral behavior.

The following are some blessings of unilateral motion:

You do now not have to enjoy gloomy and powerless; you could take charge of your conditions and your future.

By forming advantageous physical games, attitudes, and abilties, you could enhance each your relationship and your self.

By demonstrating your willpower, love, and appreciate for them, you can encourage and inspire your companion to help you in maintaining your marriage.

By fending off grievance, putting blame, and harboring anger, you can ease anxiety and conflict to your married existence.

By expressing your needs, goals, and dreams and paying attention to your partner, you could beautify conversation and fortify your bond for your marriage.

By last reliable, obedient, and encouraging, you may enhance the be given as proper with and closeness on your marriage.

You can take satisfaction to your life and your marriage through celebrating your successes, having a laugh, and being thankful.

Discuss the traumatic conditions and dangers of trying to save your marriage by myself

Saving your marriage for your very personal can be an exceptional and tough enterprise enterprise. Along the adventure, you could run into pretty some dangers and problems, like:

Experiencing discouragement and frustration. You can assume that notwithstanding your satisfactory efforts, no longer a few issue is going on. It's possible which you're thinking in case your efforts are in vain or if you're squandering your effort and time. You can end up depressed and unmotivated to go on.

Dealing with competition and rejection. Your associate won't understand or appreciate what you are doing, and you can run into opposition and rejection from them. They might also additionally criticize, steer easy of, or forget about about approximately you. They can also additionally decline to help in retaining the wedding or cooperate. They would possibly even make threats or initiate a divorce.

Becoming no longer who you're. In the direction of trying to preserve your marriage intact, you could lose sight of who you are. You could in all likelihood disregard your personal goals, opportunities, and objectives. Your morals, convictions, and obstacles is probably compromised. Your happiness, fitness, and self-worth can be at stake.

Forming unhealthful workouts and movements. While trying to keep your marriage intact, you may select up awful behavior and practices. It's viable to get clingy, needy, or obsessed. You would possibly possibly use compulsion, guilt, or manipulation. It's possible an outstanding way to self-harm, self-blame, or self-pity.

Ignoring other chances and opportunities. While looking to maintain your marriage intact, you can pass up different opportunities and opportunities.

You may skip up opportunities for professional and private improvement. You can lose out on connections and emotional and social support. You might possibly pass up distinct opportunities to accumulate contentment and pride.

Attempting to preserve your marriage on your personal gives some of troubles and dangers. They are not, however, unavoidable or insurmountable. By requesting assist and help, putting in place sound limits, maintaining an splendid outlook, and searching after yourself, you could conquer them. It's moreover viable to widely recognized and accept the bounds of your electricity and impact, and to be equipped to relinquish manipulate even as known as upon. Never neglect that there are limits to what you could do to maintain your marriage intact and that once in a while it takes to tango.

Provide practical tips and steps for starting off top notch adjustments in yourself and your courting

Making appropriate enhancements in every your courting and your self is the first step within the course of saving your marriage.

You should show in your associate which you are willing to put inside the vital try and make enhancements in each your marriage and yourself. The following useful advice and actions will help you start making superb changes on your courting and in your self:

Recognize and take away your awful conduct and moves. Consider the physical activities and moves which might be negative on your courting and your self, in conjunction with consuming, smoking, lying, or yelling. Plan to stop or reduce once more on the ones behaviors and behavior, and ask for assist if critical. Swap them out for constructive sporting activities and movements like taking walks out, analyzing, meditating, or volunteering.

Show admiration and thankfulness. Consider the factors of your relationship and yourself for which you are grateful, which incorporates your values, accomplishments, strengths, or particular reminiscences. Regularly inform yourself and your accomplice how plenty you understand and cost them, every in writing or orally. Express gratitude in your associate for their efforts in your behalf and well known their strengths and attributes.

Increase your hobby and presence of mind. Consider how you'll be plenty much less distracted, locate time for yourself, and pay attention to information in case you want to be more gift and aware about your self and your courting. By taking note of your goals and paying attention to your frame, thoughts, and emotions, you could turn out to be greater aware about being inside the 2nd with yourself.

By paying attention to what your accomplice says, does, and feels, and attending to their desires, you will be more gift and aware about them.

Try novel and captivating endeavors. Consider the topics you may do to bring life to your dating and your self, such taking on new pursuits, visiting to new areas, or studying new talents. By pursuing your pastimes, passions, or dreams and pushing yourself to develop, you may try new and thrilling subjects for your self. Plan dates, holidays, or tours together, and share your findings and reports to try new and thrilling subjects.

Provide and receive remarks. Consider the steps you may do to higher your self and your dating, collectively with providing or receiving comments or setting it into exercising. Give and accumulate comments for your self thru inquiring for and utilising other people's constructive criticism, compliments, or steerage on the manner to better yourself. Feedback on your accomplice need to take delivery of and acquired in an open, kind, and galvanizing manner. You must additionally receive and fee their input.

Emphasize the significance of staying power, staying power, and consistency

It takes time and effort to save your marriage to your own. You'll want to have some of persistence, perseverance, and consistency due to the fact there can be risks and limitations along the road. Three important developments—staying strength, tenacity, and consistency—will permit you to overcome any annoying situations or disappointments and attain your marital targets and aspirations.

The quality of persistence is the potential to undergo and control disturbing conditions, setbacks, or irritations without dropping your cool, giving up, or behaving rashly. The capability to preserve composure in the face of trouble and to behave maturely and wisely makes staying strength a precious trait. Being affected character together along with your accomplice additionally permits you to cope with them with respect and facts and prevent unneeded fights and confrontations.

The potential to keep going in your dreams and aspirations within the face of demanding situations, setbacks, or resistance is referred to as patience. Because it demonstrates your devotion and backbone to keeping your marriage and bringing approximately brilliant upgrades in each your relationship and your self, persistence is vital. Additionally, endurance allows you to triumph over your associate's competition or rejection and encourages and motivates them that will help you in keeping your marriage.

The capability to uphold and hold your sports sports and behaviors while remaining right on your goals and requirements is referred to as consistency. Being regular fosters balance and dependability for your dating as well as self guarantee and bear in mind in your partner. Additionally, retaining consistency lets in you to assess and music your overall performance in addition to make vital changes and behavioral improvements.

You can beautify your opportunities of constructing a sturdy, enjoyable, and glad connection with your accomplice and of maintaining your marriage for your private thru using workout staying power, tenacity, and consistency. Recall that it takes time, art work, and remedy in your part to keep your marriage on your very non-public.

www.ingramcontent.com/pod-product-compliance
Lightning Source LLC
Chambersburg PA
CBHW071446080526
44587CB00014B/2011